Turning Kids on to Research:
The Power of Motivation

Information Literacy Series

The Thoughtful Researcher: Teaching the Research Process to Middle School Students. By Virginia Rankin

Practical Steps to the Research Process: High School. By Deborah B. Stanley.

Fostering Information Literacy: Connecting National Standards, Goals 2000, and the SCANS Report. By Helen M. Thompson and Susan A. Henley.

Turning Kids on to Research: The Power of Motivation. By Ruth V. Small and Marilyn P. Arnone.

Pathways to Knowledge™ and Inquiry Learning. By Marjorie L. Pappas and Ann E. Tepe.

Turning Kids on to Research:
The Power of Motivation

Ruth V. Small
Marilyn P. Arnone

2000
Libraries Unlimited, Inc.
And Its Division
Teacher Ideas Press
Englewood, Colorado

Libraries Unlimited, Inc.
And Its Division Teacher Ideas Press
P.O. Box 6633
Englewood, CO 80155-6633
1-800-237-6124
www.lu.com

Library of Congress Cataloging-in-Publication Data

Small, Ruth V.
    Turning kids on to research : the power of motivation / Ruth V. Small, Marilyn P. Arnone.
        p. cm. -- (Information literacy series)
    Includes bibliographical references and index.
    ISBN 1-56308-782-0
    1. Motivation in education. 2. Research--Study and teaching. 3. Information
retrieval--Study and teaching. I. Arnone, Marilyn P. II. Title. III. Series.

LB1065.S 57 1999
370.15'4--dc21   99-050131

To all our children,
Debbie
Jackie
Alexis
Georgia
John
Missy
Scarlett
Sean
Steve

Contents

List of Figures xi
Acknowledgments xiii
Preface xv

Chapter One: Information Literacy and Motivation 1
    Introduction 2
    Scenario 2
    Information Literacy 3
    Where Does Motivation Fit In? 6
    What's Your MSQ (Motivational Style Quotient)? 7
    The Learning Audience 9
    Motivational Goals 10
    Motivational Theories 11
    Expectancy-Value Theory 12
    What Other Motivation Theories Apply? 13
        Need Theories 14
        Curiosity 16
        Flow 17
        Attribution Theory 18
        Social Learning Theory 20
        Instructional Motivation Models 21
    The Motivation Overlay for Information Skills Instruction 23
    Chapter Challenge 26
    Chapter Challenge: Answers 27
    Reflection Points 28
    References 29

Chapter Two: In the Beginning 33
    Introduction 34
    Generating Interest in the Research Process 37
    Motivational Moment 38
    Motivational Moment 41
    Motivational Moment 43
    Establishing the Importance of Information Skills 50
    Motivational Moment 51
    Motivational Moment 54
    Building Confidence in Research Ability 57
    Motivational Moment 60
    Motivational Moment 63
    What Would YOU Do? 68

Chapter Two: ... In the Beginning (*continued*)
    Motivational Makeover 69
        Lackluster Lesson Plan 70
        Ann's Motivational Makeover 72
    Chapter Challenge 75
    Chapter Challenge: Answers 76
    Reflection Points 77
    References 78

Chapter Three: ... During the Research Process 81
    Introduction 82
    Maintaining Interest in the Research Process 83
    Motivational Moment 86
    Motivational Moment 90
    Promoting the Value of Information Skills 93
    Motivational Moment 94
    Motivational Moment 97
    Reinforcing Confidence in Research Ability 99
    Motivational Moment 101
    Motivational Moment 103
    What Would YOU Do? 110
    Motivational Makeover 111
        Lackluster Lesson Plan 112
        Marilyn's Motivational Makeover 114
    Chapter Challenge 117
    Chapter Challenge: Answers 118
    Reflection Points 119
    References 120

Chapter Four: ... An Ending 123
    Introduction 124
    Encouraging Ongoing Confidence in Research Abilities 127
    Promoting Satisfaction in Research Accomplishments 131
    Motivational Moment 135
    Motivational Moment 137
    Motivational Moment 139
    Motivational Moment 140
    Motivating Continuing Information Exploration 142
    Motivational Moment 143
    What Would YOU Do? 147
    Motivational Makeover 148
        Lackluster Lesson Plan 149
        Susan's Motivational Makeover 151
    Chapter Challenge 153

Chapter Challenge: Answers 154
Reflection Points 155
References 156

Chapter Five: Putting It All Together 157
Introduction 158
Scenario Revisited 159
Creating a Constructivist Learning Environment 162
Summing Up 168
What Would YOU Do? 171
What Would YOU Do? 173
What Would YOU Do? 175
Motivational Makeover 176
    Lackluster Lesson Plan 177
    Pam's Motivational Makeover 184
Final Thoughts 187
Chapter Challenge 188
Chapter Challenge: Answers 189
Reflection Points 190
References 191

Index 193
About the Authors 199

List of Figures

Figure 1-1. Research Stages and Related Information Skills 6
Figure 1-2. Research Stages, Information Skills, and Motivational Goals 11
Figure 1-3. Presence and Absence of Value and Expectancy 13
Figure 1-4. Needs, Task Preferences, and Examples Tasks 15
Figure 1-5. The Motivation Overlay for Information Skills Instruction 24

Figure 2-1. Motivational Goal #1: Beginning Stage 37
Figure 2-2. Motivation Toolkit Goal #1: Beginning Stage 49
Figure 2-3. Motivational Goal #2: Beginning Stage 50
Figure 2-4. Concept Map: Motivation Theories and Concepts 53
Figure 2-5. Motivation Toolkit Goal #2: Beginning Stage 56
Figure 2-6. Motivational Goal #3: Beginning Stage 57
Figure 2-7. Motivation Toolkit Goal #3: Beginning Stage 65
Figure 2-8. Motivation Toolkit: Beginning Stage 66

Figure 3-1. Motivational Goal #1: During Stage 83
Figure 3-2. Motivation Toolkit Goal #1: During Stage 92
Figure 3-3. Motivational Goal #2: During Stage 92
Figure 3-4. Motivation Toolkit Goal #2: During Stage 98
Figure 3-5. Motivational Goal #3: During Stage 98
Figure 3-6. Motivation Toolkit Goal #3: During Stage 108
Figure 3-7. Motivation Toolkit: During Stage 109

Figure 4-1. Motivational Goal #1: Ending Stage 126
Figure 4-2. Motivation Toolkit Goal #1: Ending Stage 130
Figure 4-3. Motivational Goal #2: Ending Stage 131
Figure 4-4. Motivation Toolkit Goal #2: Ending Stage 141
Figure 4-5. Motivational Goal #3: Ending Stage 142
Figure 4-6. Motivation Toolkit Goal #3: Ending Stage 145
Figure 4-7. Motivation Toolkit: Ending Stage 146

Figure 5-1. Constructivist Learning Environments Are Student-Centered and
            Instructor-Facilitated 163
Figure 5-2. Constructivist Learning Environments Provide Authentic Tasks 164
Figure 5-3. Constructivist Learning Environments Demand Critical
            Thinking Skills 165
Figure 5-4. Constructivist Learning Environments Promote Student
            Interaction and Collaboration 166
Figure 5-5. Constructivist Learning Environments Foster Responsibility
            for Learning 167

Acknowledgments

This book could not have been written without the help of a number of people. We would first like to thank the practitioners who shared their stories and ideas with us and allowed us to include them in the manuscript. We would also like to thank all of our colleagues and students who generously provided us with informational feedback and motivational support during the writing process. Special thanks to Carol Kuhlthau, professor at Rutgers University, for her invaluable advice and encouragement as we began this journey; Janet LaFrance of the ERIC Clearinghouse for Information & Technology at Syracuse University for her assistance in locating hard-to-find reference materials; and Beth Mahoney for her help in preparing the final version of this manuscript. Finally, we wish to thank Joe Arnone (without whose help we might still be working on this book!) for freeing us from everyday tasks so that we could focus our efforts on the creative process.

Preface

There are many books on information problem-solving and a wealth of excellent information skills models out there. Yet few adequately address how profoundly a student's motivation can affect his or her success in learning and using information skills. There was undoubtedly a void in the professional literature, but it wasn't until two years ago that a small group of participants in our workshop on motivational techniques for information professionals urged us to spread the word to their colleagues. Thus, this book was conceived.

In the two years since then, we have learned a lot about the creative techniques that practitioners are using to motivate their students. What they lacked, however, was a systematic approach for applying motivational principles to their work. So we set upon documenting our framework for designing motivation into information skills instruction in a way that excites students about research and lifelong learning. We were not interested in inventing a new information skills model but rather in offering a way to enhance existing models with an overlay of motivational techniques and strategies. We also felt it was important to give a voice to the motivational challenges practitioners face on a daily basis and to share their many success stories.

Our framework integrates the theories of some of the leading motivational researchers with the work of Carol Kuhlthau, who has examined student motivation in the context of information literacy. In this way, we apply theory to practice for a specific target audience, those who teach information skills to young people: library media specialists, classroom teachers, and parents.

As you read this book, you will notice that each chapter builds on the content of previous chapters. You'll find a number of exercises and activities that help you review and synthesize what you have learned. We'll also challenge you with several motivational problems to solve.

We hope this book motivates you so you can, in turn, motivate your students, the information problem-solvers of the 21st century.

Chapter One

Information Literacy and Motivation

❝One of the key considerations in designing a research task
is motivation of students.❞

~ Carol Kuhlthau, 1985, p. 7

Introduction

The Chinese language is very interesting. For example, in the word below, the character on the left, when appearing by itself, means "danger" while the character on the right, when appearing by itself, means "opportunity." However, when taken together, the two characters comprise the Chinese word for "crisis."

危
Danger

机
Opportunity

危机
CRISIS

As you read the following scenario, think about how Sam's crisis situation presents him with both danger and an opportunity.

▶ **Scenario**

Sam Downey is the library media specialist at Smithville High School. During the second week of the school year, the ninth grade class pays its first visit to the library media center. When the class enters the library, the students are noisy and boisterous. Sam signals that they should sit at the tables in the instructional area of the media center but the noise level continues to elevate. Sam, yelling to be heard over the din, tells them to quiet down because he has a lot to tell them and only 30 minutes to do so.

Once the class has adequately quieted down, Sam says, "Today you will learn an information problem-solving model." One student yells out, "What's that?" Sam points to a poster on the wall, entitled "How to Complete Your Research Project," which lists steps to follow when doing research, adapted from a well-known information skills model. He says, "Later this year, you will be expected to complete a research project in your English class. This is what you will need to know." One boy remarks, "I had to do a research project in eighth grade and I got an F! Forget it—I already know I can't do this." A girl sitting nearby says, "The library media specialist at my middle school taught us this last year..." She turns to the class and adds, "... and it was *boring* then!" Another boy comments, "Who cares about this anyway? I just want to know where the science fiction books are." The class then erupts into many small discussions about the difficult and boring nature of research.

We can all agree that this somewhat extreme (but not unbelievable) scenario presents a *crisis* situation for the library media specialist (hereafter referred to as LMS). Not only has Sam lost control of this class, but he has an even larger problem. He is in *danger* of losing the interest and involvement of these students because of their low motivation toward the learning task. However, Sam also has a wonderful *opportunity*. With some thoughtful planning and a little creativity, Sam can teach the research process in a way that is fun, exciting, and meaningful to these students. Keep Sam's situation in mind as you read this book. We'll return to the scenario later.

Effective information literacy programs not only help students acquire the skills they will need to explore their world and solve their information problems, but also stimulate intellectual curiosity, encourage a desire for continued information seeking, and promote a lifelong love of learning. That's where motivation comes in. This book offers practitioners a framework for accomplishing these motivational goals by systematically applying effective motivational techniques to their information skills lessons. By the end of Chapter One, you will:

◆ understand the relationship between information literacy and motivation

◆ describe several important motivation theories

◆ have a working understanding of the Motivation Overlay designed for information skills instruction

Information Literacy

The Final Report of the American Library Association (ALA) Presidential Committee on Information Literacy describes the information-literate citizen as one who "must be able to recognize when information is needed and have the ability to locate, evaluate and use effectively the needed information" (1989, p. 1). To be information-literate is to be "an effective user of ideas and information," according to *Information Power: Building Partnerships for Learning*, the professional guidelines for the school library field (AASL and AECT, 1998, p. 6). Doyle (1992) defines information literacy as "the ability to access, evaluate, and use information from a variety of sources" (p. 1). It is what we need to do, according to Eisenberg and Lowe (1997), "to prepare students for success in the age of information" (p. 23).

The research on information literacy suggests that information skills be taught as process and integrated with the curriculum (Plotnick, 1999). Several information problem-solving models have been developed in recent years to help guide the development of instruction that teaches young people the skills they need to be information-literate citizens. It is assumed you, the reader, are at least somewhat familiar with many, if not all, of these models, so we only briefly review a few of them below.

Eisenberg and Berkowitz's Big Six Approach to Information Problem-Solving (1990) specifies a general approach to the information problem-solving process consisting of six major steps. The Big Six Approach begins with defining the parameters of the information task or problem and ends with evaluating both the results of the process and the process itself.

Stripling and Pitts's Research Process Model (1988) follows a more linear approach to research, a 10-step process interspersed with eight "reflection points" that allow students to evaluate and revise or repeat completed steps where needed.

The Information Problem-Solving Skills model, developed by the Wisconsin Educational Media Association (WEMA) and adopted by the American Association of School Librarians (1993) is also linear and, like the others, progresses from defining an information need to evaluating the product and process.

Pappas and Tepe's "Follett Information Skills Model" (1995) uses a graphical format to convey a nonlinear approach to the information-seeking process. A unique feature of their model is an initial "Appreciation" stage that focuses on the role of curiosity in motivating an information need.

Yucht's Flip-It! Model (1997) presents a generic information problem-solving process. This model uses an "if/then" approach that encourages students to link the research task to their previous learning.

Kuhlthau's Model of the Search Process (1993) uses the results of several years of research to describe the six stages that students undergo during the research process. She found that, rather than a neat and sequential set of skills, it is a learning process that can be somewhat messy and more iterative in nature; for example, students often explore and collect information before they have formulated or narrowed a topic or, where they formulate a topic, explore information about the topic, refine their topic, explore more information, and so on. Through her work,

Kuhlthau has identified the cognitive strategies and affective feelings that students experience at various stages in the research process.

In general, all of these models share a common framework that we have synthesized into eight major categories of information skills, sequenced across three broad research stages as shown below.

Beginning Stage:

Definition

- ◆ The student defines the information need or task and articulates his or her goal.

Selection

- ◆ The student begins the process of identifying a research topic or question to be explored.

Planning

- ◆ The student formulates an information search strategy, identifying a range of potential, relevant types of information sources to be explored.

During Stage:

Exploration

- ◆ The student accesses, uses, and explores a range of information resources and finalizes formulation of a research topic or question.

Collection

- ◆ The student gathers and makes note of relevant information from various sources.

Organization

- ◆ The student summarizes, sequences, and synthesizes gathered information.

Ending Stage:

Presentation

- ◆ The student communicates the results in the form of a presentation or report.

Evaluation

- ◆ The student evaluates both the product and the process to determine whether the information goal has been achieved and ways to improve future research activities.

It must be emphasized that these stages and skills are not intended to infer a lockstep linear process but rather an iterative process in which any or all skills may be revisited in order to modify or expand on previous ones. This is particularly true during the Beginning and During Stages when, as Kuhlthau found, students may feel apprehensive and uncertain and are more likely to become discouraged. For example, the student may need to spend time browsing some information resources before having enough knowledge to be able to pinpoint a research topic or formulate a research question. Or, while exploring information resources on a selected research topic, the student may find types or amounts of information that require some expansion, modification, or even a change in that topic.

The research stages and information skills are summarized in the figure below.

Figure 1-1. Research Stages and Related Information Skills

Research Stages	Beginning	During	Ending
Information Skills	Definition Selection Planning	Exploration Collection Organization	Presentation Evaluation

Where Does Motivation Fit In?

Before reading about some of the motivational concepts and theories related to the stages and information skills presented previously, it might be fun for you to complete the following brief questionnaire to assess your MSQ (Motivational Style Quotient). You may want to write your responses on a separate piece of paper so you can refer back to them as we discuss each of the motivation theories throughout this chapter.

What's Your MSQ (Motivational Style Quotient)?

Rate each of the following statements describing your information skills lessons using the following scale:

2 = Often	1 = Sometimes	0 = Never

_____ 1. I link the learning of information skills to classroom assignments and curricular activities or to students' personal needs or interests.

_____ 2. I provide research tasks that are challenging but attainable.

_____ 3. I offer information services and resources for enrichment to students who seek opportunities to explore topics of interest.

_____ 4. I incorporate group exercises or group projects into my information skills instruction.

_____ 5. I provide activities in which students who have mastered the research process can help other students attain mastery.

_____ 6. I use questions or surprising statements to trigger the need to explore information.

_____ 7. I inject uncertainty, incongruity, or mystery into my information skills lcssons.

_____ 8. I ensure students have adequate time and guidance for using information resources and technologies to complete their research projects.

_____ 9. I encourage students to assume responsibility for becoming information literate.

_____10. I break down my information skills instruction into small, manageable chunks so that all students can achieve with success.

_____11. I provide encouragement and praise to students when they show progress in learning information skills.

_____12. I model enthusiasm for using library and information skills.

_____ **TOTAL SCORE**

Now total your ratings for all 12 MSQ items. If you scored between 19 and 24, you're already a super motivator, but keep reading because you may pick up some new ideas for motivating your students. If you scored between 13 and 18, you are incorporating several motivational strategies into your information skills instruction but there is still room for improvement. In the following chapters, you will find a wide selection of motivational techniques and example strategies from which to choose (based on what fits your style and needs). If you scored 12 or less, you may be feeling hampered due to time constraints, lack of support, or other obstacles to achieving a higher MSQ. The motivational techniques and strategies presented in this book are easy to apply and require no special resources.

This book gives you a framework for developing a more systematic approach to designing motivational information skills lessons and provides a wealth of great ideas suggested by your colleagues that are easy and inexpensive to implement. As you read the rest of this chapter, you'll learn more about each of the MSQ questions and the motivational theories upon which they are based.

> "Why do I have to learn this?"
>
> "This is so boring!"
>
> "See, I told you I couldn't learn this!"

Sound familiar? Most educators have heard these or similar comments at one time or another from their students. LMSs are no exception, often encountering such comments while meeting with groups or individual students to teach or review the information problem-solving process. An understanding of their motivation (why our students behave the way they do) allows us to then focus on making what they do and how they do it more meaningful and enjoyable. This accomplishes part of *Information Power*'s stated mission "by providing instruction to foster competence and stimulate interest in reading, viewing, and using information and ideas" (p. 6).

While current information literacy models do a great job of describing the appropriate concepts and skills to be taught, they (with the possible exceptions of Carol Kuhlthau's work and Pappas and Tepe's acknowledgment of the role of curiosity as an information need motivator) largely ignore the motivational side of information skills instruction—they *describe* what to teach, but do not *prescribe* a systematic method for teaching it in a way that incorporates specific motivational techniques.

As information professionals, we have a special responsibility for getting students excited about using information resources, services, and technologies to solve information problems and stimulating a desire to seek and gain knowledge, something we call "information motivation." Information motivation begins with knowing your learning audience.

The Learning Audience

Kuhlthau (1991) studied the thoughts, feelings, and behaviors of students as they proceeded through the research process. She found that students experience a number of emotions that affect their attitudes and motivation. For example, she describes the "exploration stage" of research as the most difficult, when students encounter information that is inconsistent or incompatible with what they already know, resulting in feelings of anxiety, uncertainty, and low confidence. It is not until about midway through the process that students begin to resolve this uncertainty, formulate a more precise topic and search strategy, and feel more confident and self-determining.

So, it is essential that you think carefully about your specific learning audience (i.e., their incoming feelings, attitudes, and motives) *before* selecting motivational strategies for your information skills lessons. Some questions you might want to consider asking yourself are:

◆ Do your students see value in learning research skills?

◆ Are your students excited about information exploration and knowledge seeking?

◆ Do your students believe they have the information skills and knowledge needed to successfully complete a research task?

If you answered no to any of these questions, you are faced with a motivational challenge.

Before you can begin to prescribe appropriate motivational techniques for your students, it is important to diagnose their incoming motivation as precisely as possible.

Once you understand their motivation, the obvious next question is, "So what can I do about it?" This book attempts to answer this question by building on and linking the work of Kuhlthau and others on information literacy with several theorists on motivation. We begin by identifying a set of overall motivational goals related to the stages and skills previously described and discuss several relevant theories that form the theoretical underpinnings of our "Motivation Overlay for Information Skills Instruction," which is described in detail later in this chapter. (We'll also reveal how your responses to each of the MSQ questions relate to this discussion.)

Motivational Goals

You have probably formulated a number of instructional goals when designing your information skills lessons. *Instructional* goals use broad statements to describe the intended results (generally cognitive) of your instruction. Some examples of instructional goals are:

◆ Students will learn some sources where they might find the information needed for their assignment.

◆ Students will be able to evaluate information sources.

Motivational goals, on the other hand, describe general feelings, attitudes, and motives you hope to achieve through your instruction and are a prerequisite to the selection, and later evaluation, of effective motivational techniques. We have identified several critical motivational goals for each of the research stages and information skills. These goals are not intended to *replace* your instructional goals; rather they are meant to *enrich* them.

As you read the following description of these goals, you should think about ways to assess them. Motivational assessment measures are typically less well defined than learning assessment measures, as motivation is less easily quantifiable than learning. Examples of methods for measuring achievement of motivational goals are observation, discussion, and self-report measures.

When students begin the information problem-solving process and identify their learning task and its parameters, it is important to find ways to (1) generate student interest in the research process, (2) establish the importance of learning information skills, and (3) build the student's confidence in his/her ability to acquire information skills and complete the research task by using appropriate information resources and technologies. As students explore, gather, and organize information, motivational goals focus on (1) maintaining their interest in the research process, (2) promoting the value of using information skills, and (3) reinforcing their confidence in their ability to apply those skills to a variety of information problems.

Finally, as students proceed through the concluding phases of the process in which the research results must be presented and evaluated, motivational goals focus on (1) encouraging ongoing confidence in an ability to use their information skills, (2) promoting a sense of satisfaction in their research accomplishments, and (3) stimulating a continuing motivation to explore information resources and solve information problems. The figure below summarizes the relationship among the motivational goals, research stages, and information skills.

Motivational Theories

Figure 1-2. Research Stages, Information Skills, and Motivational Goals

Research Stages	Beginning	During	Ending
Information Skills	Definition Selection Planning	Exploration Collection Organization	Presentation Evaluation
Motivational Goals	Generate interest in the research process. Establish importance of information skills. Build confidence in research ability.	Maintain interest in the research process. Promote value of information skills. Reinforce confidence in research ability.	Encourage ongoing confidence in research ability. Promote satisfaction in research accomplishments. Motivate continuing information exploration.

While there are several motivation theories that are relevant to an information literacy context, we have chosen expectancy-value (E-V) theory (e.g., Vroom, 1964) as the primary theoretical foundation. We also describe several other theories that we consider important in this context.

Expectancy-Value Theory

E-V theory has been applied over the past 30 years to a variety of contexts, including workplace management (e.g., Vroom, 1964) and classroom teaching (e.g., Miskel et al., 1980). We believe it is equally applicable to an information literacy context. E-V theory suggests that there are two major motives that influence whether a person will put forth effort when faced with a task. The first motive is **value**; the person must recognize something of personal interest or meaning in achieving the task. By helping students see the importance of acquiring information skills by offering services that add value to their research tasks or that satisfy personal needs or interests, you address MSQ #1. Examples of ways to do this are:

- ◆ tying information skills instruction to a specific class assignment
- ◆ bookmarking high-quality websites that relate to students' research topics

The second motive of E-V theory is the **expectancy for success**; a person must have the expectation that he or she can be successful at a given task, that he or she is capable of doing what is necessary to accomplish a goal. By helping students acquire competence for using information resources and technologies for achieving appropriately challenging research tasks (MSQ #2), you are promoting students' expectations for success. Appropriately challenging research tasks are those that provide adequate challenge to keep students interested enough to persist, but not too much challenge to cause them to become frustrated and discouraged and to give up. While young children often maintain high expectations for success (even when experiencing repeated failure), this is not so for older children, who often associate failure (particularly when effort is high) with a lack of ability (Lumsden, 1994). They tend to believe that the reason they don't learn is that they're not capable of learning. There are many ways to help promote students' expectations for success, several of which we will describe in the following chapters of this book.

In addition to the student believing that he or she is capable, *you* must believe it. Deborah Stipek writes, "To a very large degree, students expect to learn if their teachers expect them to learn" (1988, p. 209). We come to every instructional situation with certain expectations about an individual or group of students. Research indicates that when we approach all learners with high (but attainable) expectations, our students will try hard to live up to those expectations. And, of course, the opposite is also true; when we believe that a group or individual cannot learn, this prediction becomes a self-fulfilling prophecy. It is important to maintain high expectations and an encouraging atmosphere throughout the research process.

One of the most important things for you to remember about expectancy-value theory is that it requires attention to *both* factors (value and expectation for success). If you incorporate motivational techniques into your information skills lessons that help students recognize the value in learning the research process, but don't help them to know they are capable of learning the information skills needed to successfully complete that process (or vice versa), it is likely that you will do little to motivate your students.

It might be useful to think about this in a formulaic way.

Figure 1-3. Presence and Absence of Value and Expectancy

Value	x	Expectancy	=	Motivation
No	x	No	=	No
Yes	x	No	=	No
No	x	Yes	=	No
Yes	x	Yes	=	YES!

While the foundation for our work is expectancy-value theory, there are a number of other motivation theories that we also consider. We describe these theories in the next section.

What Other Motivation Theories Apply?

There are several motivation theories (many of which are relevant to expectancy-value theory) that help further explain student motivation (or lack of it) toward learning information skills and suggest how to respond, instructionally speaking. Some theories are applicable at any time throughout the research process, while others are better suited to one or two stages. Need theories are most applicable to the Beginning Stage of the research process, when students enter the learning situation with certain needs and attitudes that influence their information problem-solving behavior. Therefore, we address these theories first.

Need Theories

When we address student needs, we are plugging into the value component of E-V theory. That is, students will value the learning experience more if it directly addresses their personal needs.

There are several theories that focus on human needs, but perhaps the most recognizable is Abraham Maslow's Hierarchy of Needs (1943). Maslow identified five categories of needs that are hierarchical in nature (i.e., each preceding level of need must be considered before aiming at the next higher-level need). The five categories of needs range from basic physiological and safety needs to acceptance and self-esteem, and finally to realizing one's potential to the fullest degree (what Maslow calls "self-actualization").

Maslow's theory is as applicable today as it was when it was first introduced over 50 years ago. In an information literacy context, for example, it may provide more of a challenge for you to engage students in learning information skills if they come to the library media center just before lunch when their stomachs are growling and their thoughts are fixated on pizza and chocolate milk. This responds to the lower levels of Maslow's hierarchy.

As we move students to higher levels, you can contribute to creating an atmosphere of acceptance by providing a supportive learning environment in which students feel it is safe to make mistakes, try new ideas, and express opinions. This is especially important for adolescents who have a strong need to preserve their self-esteem and attain peer approval. You can contribute to building the self-esteem of students by helping them gain competence—to learn the skills they need to become competent information problem solvers and intrinsically motivated information seekers.

In 1961, building on the work of Maslow and other need theorists, David McClelland published his theory of achievement motivation. Achievement motivation identifies three important universal needs. These needs are:

- *need for achievement* (a need to attain a level of personal excellence)
- *need for affiliation* (a need to find opportunities for social interaction)
- *need for power* (a need to have an impact on others)

Students with a *high need for achievement* prefer independent, moderately challenging learning tasks. They strive to achieve their personal best. High-need-for-achievement students often seek out learning challenges and opportunities to go beyond the tasks assigned to them, frequently with greater energy and creativity. Therefore, your response to MSQ #3 describes whether you provide an information-rich environment in which students high in need for achievement have access to the information they need and want. Some examples of enrichment activities are:

◆ giving students a list of books and websites on a topic of interest

◆ providing additional projects or activities the students can pursue

◆ allowing students to extend their current projects or develop them in innovative ways

Students *high in need for affiliation* favor activities that allow them opportunities to interact with other students. This corresponds to MSQ #4. By designing opportunities for group activities or projects into your information skills lessons (e.g., forming cooperative learning teams to  complete an oral history project), you address the affiliation needs of your students. There is evidence that as a result of working in cooperative learning groups, students have stronger beliefs that they are liked, supported, and accepted by other students (Johnson and Johnson, 1987).

Students with a *high need for power* prefer activities in which they can assume leadership roles and influence others. They enjoy competitive activities and opportunities to direct others. One way to help satisfy the need for power is by encouraging students who have mastered the research process to help other students attain mastery (MSQ #5), as for example, in a peer tutoring situation.

Figure 1-4. Needs, Task Preferences, and Examples Tasks

High Need	Task Preference	Example Task
Achievement	Challenging	Independent research project
Affiliation	Interactive	Team project
Power	Influential	Peer tutoring

McClelland's three types of needs may be summarized as follows:

We have described several types of needs that students may have before, during, and even after learning the research process. Each of these needs, when satisfied, adds value to the learning experience and increases its relevance to students.

Satisfying students' personal needs is one of the essential building blocks for achieving the ultimate motivational goal of information literacy instruction: to foster students' intrinsic motivation to learn and explore their world through information. Another critical approach requires stimulating and sustaining their curiosity, a theory that we address next.

Curiosity

Curiosity may have killed the cat but it is an essential characteristic of an information-literate person. Often we need to explore our environment in order to resolve some uncertainty or cognitive conflict, what Loewenstein referred to as an "information gap" (1994). Sometimes this need is stimulated by our "curiosity." Daniel Berlyne, a pioneer in curiosity research, describes curiosity as a state of arousal brought about by complex stimuli and uncertainty in the environment, leading to exploratory behavior (1960). "With the current emphasis on constructivist learning environments, curiosity plays an important role in determining the type and amount of learning and exploration in which a learner chooses to engage and is an important factor in promoting an intrinsic motivation to learn" (Small and Arnone, 1998).

Berlyne described *epistemic* curiosity as curiosity that can only be resolved through the acquisition of knowledge. The use of thought-provoking questions or surprising statements can trigger students' epistemic curiosity and information exploration, corresponding to MSQ #6. Presenting a stimulus with a moderate degree of uncertainty, incongruity, or mystery creates curiosity and an interest in resolving the uncertainty by engaging in information exploration, corresponding to MSQ #7. However, too much uncertainty (e.g., failing to help students narrow their research topics so they end up receiving hundreds of citations in response to a research query) can result in feeling overwhelmed and anxious; while too little stimulation (e.g., repeating the same class exercise over and over) can result in disinterest and boredom. Either of these extremes is likely to cause a withdrawal from any exploratory behaviors associated with curiosity and a decrease in intrinsic motivation. Your responses to MSQ #6 and MSQ #7 reflect how well you are fostering students' curiosity and promoting an intrinsic motivation for research and information exploration.

Intrinsic motivation is closely related to school achievement and perceptions of academic competence. Some students seem to almost always be intrinsically motivated to learn. For them, participating in the learning activity is all that's needed to stimulate their curiosity and interest and promote feelings of competence or control over their own learning (e.g., Gottfried, 1985). An intrinsically motivated person is one who undertakes a task or participates in an activity because the task or activity is motivating by itself, and successfully accomplishing that task or completing that activity is the desired end result. We can promote an intrinsic motivation for becoming information literate by tying students' learning successes to their hard work and mastery of information skills, as shown in MSQ #7.

The ultimate form of intrinsic motivation may be reflected in a phenomenon called "flow." We discuss this phenomenon in the next section.

Flow

Csiksentmihalyi (1990) describes a flow experience as one that occurs when you intensely focus attention on a specific activity and become so completely immersed in that activity that you lose track of time and space. Flow epitomizes a state of heightened curiosity and intrinsic motivation.

Both children and adults experience flow. You have probably experienced flow at one time or another, perhaps when completing a challenging jigsaw puzzle, playing a computer game, reading a book, or creating a display. Flow can occur during any type of activity (Csiksentmihalyi found the phenomenon in people during such different activities as playing chess, doing construction, and ballet dancing), so long as it provides an appropriate level of challenge, stimulates curiosity, clearly defines goals, and offers immediate and useful feedback on progress toward a goal. Researchers have found a positive relationship between flow and exploratory behavior. In an information context, a flow situation would require adequate time and resources. Therefore, providing opportunities for students to spend an extended time in the library media center to work on their research projects is one way of offering a learning environment that facilitates flow (MSQ #8) and helps to increase their intrinsic motivation.

But what about those students who don't appear to be intrinsically motivated—those who only engage in a learning activity if provided with some type of external reward, such as praise or a prize? These students are said to be "extrinsically motivated"; they generally undertake a task or participate in an activity in order to receive the reward. The reward becomes the desired end rather than the means to successfully achieve the task or complete the activity. These students may often display boredom, indifference, and negative attitudes toward learning in general and information skills in particular. Some of the reasons for this extrinsic orientation may be better understood once you have read the following section on attribution theory.

Attribution Theory

Attribution theory (e.g.,Weiner, 1972) proposes that a person will assign one of four (two internal, two external) explanations to his or her success or failure at a task. The two internalized attributions are:

- ◆ **ability** (e.g., "I succeeded because I know how to use an online database" or "I failed because I haven't learned how to narrow an online search")
- ◆ **effort** (e.g., "I succeeded because I worked hard on my research project" or "I failed because I did not put forth enough effort on my final presentation")

The two external explanations are:

- ◆ **task difficulty** (e.g., "I succeeded because the class exercise was so easy" or "I failed because the test was too difficult")
- ◆ **luck** (e.g., "I did well on that project because I was wearing my lucky green hat" or "Mr. X really doesn't like me. That's why I got a poor grade")

These internal and external attributions are related to a perceived locus of control (e.g., Rotter 1966). If a student feels she can control a situation, she is said to have an internal locus of control and is more likely to have internal attributions. However, if a student believes he has no control over his own fate, he is said to have an external locus of control and will probably attribute outcomes in terms of external forces. Your response to MSQ #9 demonstrates how well you are promoting a more internal attribution by encouraging students to take more responsibility for their own learning success or failure.

Brophy (1986) describes a process called "attribution retraining" for use with students who are discouraged about their ability to learn. He advocates helping students to: (1) focus on the task at hand rather than dwelling on past failures; (2) review their work to identify mistakes or alternative ways to approach the learning task; and (3) attribute their failure to a lack of effort, insufficient information, or use of ineffective learning strategies.

Motivational techniques that promote intrinsic motivation and internal attributions are likely to influence positive attitudes toward information exploration and the research process. We must caution, however, that there are times when it is *inappropriate* for students to have an internal attribution (e.g., "I can't learn this because I'm not smart enough") and times when it is *appropriate* to have an external attribution, for example when the task *really is* at a level too easy or too difficult for that student.

Students who (1) experience repeated failure, (2) do not perceive their actions as influencing their failures, and (3) consistently attribute negative outcomes to external forces may develop a condition known as "learned helplessness" (e.g., Seligman, 1975). Learned-helpless people believe they have no control over a situation and perceive that no matter what they do, they will fail. So they just give up—they don't make any effort, even when there is clearly an opportunity for success. (We saw an example of learned helplessness in our Scenario earlier in this chapter.)

Learned helplessness is often the result of repeated early failures. An effective technique for preventing learned helplessness is to break your information skills instruction (particularly those concepts or skills that are new or abstract) into small, manageable chunks of information that students can understand and learn (corresponding to MSQ #10). Some other techniques for preventing learned helplessness are:

- ◆ finding ways to show students the relevance of the research task
- ◆ encouraging students
- ◆ providing specific feedback on how to improve performance

Although we certainly would like all of our students to be intrinsically motivated all of the time, the truth is that a student is rarely intrinsically motivated *all* the time. Think about it: aren't there times when you need some external reward—when the challenge or thrill of learning for its own sake is just not enough? But don't worry; even extrinsic motivators can encourage intrinsic motivation *if* they are a direct result of accomplishing the learning task. For example, a field trip to see a local production of *Hamlet* would be an appropriate type of extrinsic reward for students who had successfully completed research projects on Shakespeare's plays because it is relevant to the task, and enhancing learning is the desired end. Having a pizza party to celebrate completion of the same projects, although not an inappropriate reward, will do little to promote a continuing intrinsic motivation to learn because the party is totally unrelated to the learning task and the party itself becomes the desired end. In situations where students are learning something unfamiliar or difficult, any extrinsic rewards valued by the students may be effective motivators in the short term (particularly with underachievers). Providing encouragement and praise to all students as they make progress toward achieving learning goals is one of the most powerful techniques for fostering continuing motivation. Give yourself a "gold star" if you answered "often" to MSQ #11. How students attribute their learning successes and failures has a direct impact on their ongoing expectations for successful learning experiences.

The last theory we describe, social learning theory, has two elements that we feel are particularly well suited to designing motivating information skills lessons. They are modeling and reinforcement. Each is explained in the next section.

Social Learning Theory

Social learning theory (e.g., Bandura, 1982) promotes the effectiveness of learning from direct experience, observation, and modeled behavior. Modeled behavior can come from real-life observations of people (e.g., parents, teachers, LMSs, other students) or vicarious observations through instructions or directions (e.g., a computer-based simulation) and/or from visual representations (e.g., a television show). All three of these types of models may be used by LMSs to motivate learning of the research process. For example, the LMS can demonstrate appropriate information skills, verbalize aloud the steps to be taken, provide a handout that summarizes the steps in the research process, and show a videotape of students completing various stages of the research process.

American essayist and poet Ralph Waldo Emerson once wrote, "Nothing great was ever achieved without enthusiasm." One avenue for school library media specialists to channel their enthusiasm, according to *Information Power*, is through the "enthusiastic use of books, videos, films, multimedia, and other creative expressions of information as sources of pleasure and information" (AASL and AECT, 1998, p. 67). Another effective outlet for demonstrating your enthusiasm is using information skills (MSQ #12). This enthusiasm can be contagious with your students, so don't be shy about expressing your exuberance for research and information exploration!

Reinforcement is another critical component of social learning theory. Reinforcement is often external (e.g., providing direct reinforcement to a student's behavior or attitude or providing vicarious reinforcement that the student observes). While positive external reinforcements can be of limited effectiveness, self-reinforcement fosters self-determination and intrinsic motivation because the student is in control and determines his or her own standard for success. Only then can students develop into critical and independent users of information and ideas. Reinforcement is an important factor in the two instructional motivation models briefly described in the next section.

Instructional Motivation Models

There are two well-known and widely implemented instructional motivation models that have influenced our work. Raymond Wlodkowski developed the Time Continuum Model (e.g., 1984), a model that identifies student motivation needs along the time continuum of an instructional event (e.g., lesson, unit). This model specifies that students enter the learning experience with certain attitudes and needs (we call this their "motivational profile"), which need to be addressed in the instructional design. Once students become involved in the learning process, they require continuing stimulation in order to remain motivated. As students conclude the learning process, they expect to attain competence and receive reinforcement.

These three time periods (Beginning, During, and Ending) require distinctively different instructional interventions, as Kuhlthau's work has also indicated.

John Keller's ARCS Model of Motivational Design (e.g., 1987) is a model based primarily on expectancy-value theory. The ARCS Model is one of the best known and most widely implemented general motivational design models for classroom instruction. The ARCS Model is an easy-to-apply, heuristic approach to increasing the motivational appeal of instruction. The model identifies four essential components of motivating instruction:

◆ **A**ttention—the instructor uses strategies for arousing and sustaining curiosity and interest, such as novelty and incongruity, questions and problems, and varied teaching methods and media.

◆ **R**elevance—the instructor links the various components of instruction (e.g., objectives, content, assessment) to the students' needs, interests, and motives.

◆ **C**onfidence—the instructor helps students develop a positive expectation for successful achievement of a learning task by sharing learning goals, providing challenges at the appropriate level, and connecting success in learning with effort.

◆ **S**atisfaction—the instructor manages extrinsic and intrinsic reinforcement by providing a supportive learning environment, supplying positive reinforcement and feedback when appropriate.

The ARCS Model is a simple, yet powerful *instructional motivation model* and provides an excellent foundation for extending Keller's work to the information arena. The ARCS Model was used as a framework for analyzing the results of a study by Small (1999) that investigated the types of motivational strategies used by elementary and middle school library media specialists in their information skills teaching. The analysis indicates that these library media specialists:

◆ predominantly use attention strategies, particularly questioning strategies.

◆ use many extrinsic motivators, most of which are related to the learning task.

◆ use few intrinsic motivators.

In general, the study found that library media specialists lack a systematic approach to designing motivation into their information skills instruction. The Motivation Overlay for Information Skills Instruction is intended to provide such an approach.

The Motivation Overlay for Information Skills Instruction

We have described the research stages and related information skills (IS), explained the importance of knowing the incoming needs and motivations of your learning audience, provided a set of motivational goals, and reviewed several related motivation theories that form the theoretical basis for our Motivation Overlay for Information Skills Instruction (or "Motivation Overlay" for short). We call it an "overlay" because it is a layer to be superimposed upon existing information skills models in order to guide the creation or selection of motivational techniques in your information skills lessons. Thus, we are not promoting one particular IS model over another but suggesting an overlay to whichever model you are already using or feel comfortable with.

The Motivation Overlay is specifically designed to meet the instruction needs of school LMSs and classroom teachers in the K–12 environment. The Motivation Overlay promotes an *information motivation* perspective to (1) excite students about information exploration and knowledge discovery, and (2) encourage self-determination and self-efficacy in knowledge seeking by helping students develop information literacy competence for lifelong learning.

The Motivation Overlay prescribes an SOS (situation-outcomes-strategies) framework for creating challenging, student-centered, information-rich learning environments that (1) take into account the motivational *situation*, including the incoming motivational profile (attitudes and motives) of students; (2) target desired motivational *outcomes*; and (3) suggest broad motivational techniques and specific *strategies* to engage learners in and excite them about the process of constructing meaningful knowledge and developing skills in order to solve authentic information. The Motivation Overlay for Information Skills Instruction appears on page 24.

The next three chapters of this book take you through each of the stages of the research process, weaving in the motivational goals and theories described in this chapter and suggesting a variety of broad motivational techniques and specific example strategies that may be incorporated into your information skills lessons. Chapters Two, Three, and Four include:

◆ a "Motivation Toolkit" that identifies dozens of useful motivational techniques and strategies for planning, repairing, and enhancing information skills lessons at specific stages in the process

Figure 1-5. The Motivation Overlay for Information Skills Instruction

Research Stages	Beginning	During	Ending
Information Skills	Definition Selection Planning	Exploration Collection Organization	Presentation Evaluation
Motivational Goals	Generate interest in the research process. Establish importance of information skills. Build confidence in research ability.	Maintain interest in the research process. Promote value of information skills. Reinforce confidence in research ability.	Encourage ongoing confidence in research ability. Promote satisfaction in research accomplishments. Motivate continuing information exploration.
Related Motivational Theories	Expectancy-value Need Curiosity Attribution Social learning	Expectancy-value Need Flow Attribution Social learning	Expectancy-value Attribution Curiosity Social learning

◆ a variety of exercises to challenge your learning

◆ real-life anecdotes of motivational situations, outcomes, and strategies "in action" submitted by LMSs and teachers

◆ examples of lackluster information skills lessons transformed through the use of effective motivational techniques

Our final chapter briefly looks at ways in which the concepts and principles presented in this book contribute to the development of a constructivist learning environment within the library media center, and provides a summary of key points and some exercises that will help you synthesize various concepts presented throughout this book, including a return to Sam Downey and his group of rowdy ninth graders described in the Scenario at the beginning of this chapter. We have purposefully chosen a practical, interactive approach and encourage you to use and reuse any or all of the suggested motivational strategies and techniques to ensure the motivational quality of your information skills lessons and promote a love of research and lifelong learning in your students.

On the next page (and at the end of each chapter in this book), you will find a "Chapter Challenge," a set of questions that test your knowledge about the content covered in the chapter. We hope you will use the Chapter Challenge as a way to review and reinforce several of the important concepts covered in the chapter.

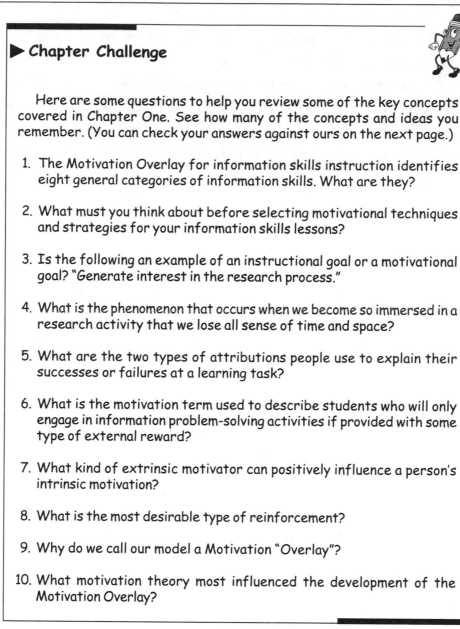

▶ Chapter Challenge

Here are some questions to help you review some of the key concepts covered in Chapter One. See how many of the concepts and ideas you remember. (You can check your answers against ours on the next page.)

1. The Motivation Overlay for information skills instruction identifies eight general categories of information skills. What are they?

2. What must you think about before selecting motivational techniques and strategies for your information skills lessons?

3. Is the following an example of an instructional goal or a motivational goal? "Generate interest in the research process."

4. What is the phenomenon that occurs when we become so immersed in a research activity that we lose all sense of time and space?

5. What are the two types of attributions people use to explain their successes or failures at a learning task?

6. What is the motivation term used to describe students who will only engage in information problem-solving activities if provided with some type of external reward?

7. What kind of extrinsic motivator can positively influence a person's intrinsic motivation?

8. What is the most desirable type of reinforcement?

9. Why do we call our model a Motivation "Overlay"?

10. What motivation theory most influenced the development of the Motivation Overlay?

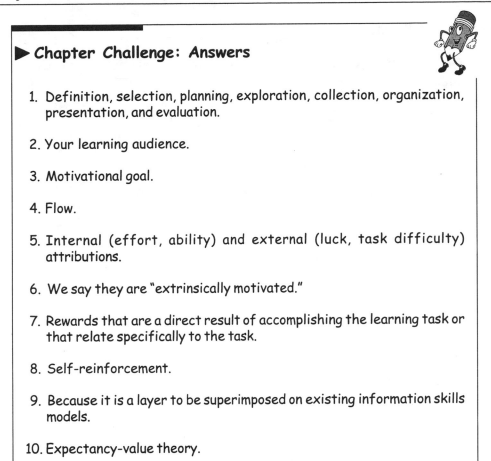

▶ **Chapter Challenge: Answers**

1. Definition, selection, planning, exploration, collection, organization, presentation, and evaluation.

2. Your learning audience.

3. Motivational goal.

4. Flow.

5. Internal (effort, ability) and external (luck, task difficulty) attributions.

6. We say they are "extrinsically motivated."

7. Rewards that are a direct result of accomplishing the learning task or that relate specifically to the task.

8. Self-reinforcement.

9. Because it is a layer to be superimposed on existing information skills models.

10. Expectancy-value theory.

Reflection Points

Please use this page to record your ideas and the special points you wish to remember from Chapter One.

References

AASL and AECT, *Information Power: Building Partnerships for Learning* (Chicago: American Library Association, 1998).

AASL and WEMA, *Information Literacy: A Position Paper on Information Problem-Solving* (Chicago: AASL, 1993).

American Library Association Presidential Committee on Information Literacy, *Final Report* (Chicago: American Library Association [ED 315 074], 1989).

Bandura, Albert, "Self-Efficacy Mechanism in Human Agency," *American Psychologist* 37, no. 2 (1982): 122-147.

Berlyne, Daniel. E., *Conflict, Arousal, and Curiosity* (New York: McGraw-Hill Book Company, 1960).

Brophy, Jere, "On Motivating Students," *Occasional Paper No. 101* (East Lansing, MI: Institute for Research on Teaching [ED 276 724], Oct. 1986).

Csiksentmihalyi, Mihalyi, *Flow: The Psychology of Optimal Experience* (New York: Harper & Row, 1990).

Doyle, Christina A., *Final Report to the National Forum on Information Literacy* (Syracuse, NY: ERIC Clearinghouse on Information and Technology [ED 351 033], 1992).

Eisenberg, Michael E., and Robert E. Berkowitz, *Information Problem-Solving: The Big Six Skills Approach to Library and Information Skills Instruction* (Norwood, NJ: Ablex, 1990).

Eisenberg, Michael E., and Carrie A. Lowe, "The Big 6 Skills: Looking at the World Through Information Problem-Solving Glasses," in *Instructional Interventions for Information Use* (Troutdale, OR: Proceedings of the Treasure Mountain Research Retreat VI, 1997): 23.

Emerson, Ralph Waldo. "Circles," in *Essays and Lectures,* edited by Joel Porte (Cambridge: Cambridge University Press/Library of America 15, 1983), 414.

Gottfried, A.E., "Academic Intrinsic Motivation in Elementary and Junior High School Students," *Journal of Educational Psychology* 77, no. 6 (1985): 631-645.

Johnson, D.W., and R.T. Johnson, *A Meta-Analysis of Cooperative, Competitive, and Individualistic Goal Structures* (Hillsdale, NJ: Erlbaum, 1987).

Keller, John M., "The Systematic Process of Motivational Design," *Performance & Instruction* (1987): 1-8.

Kuhlthau, Carol, "A Process Approach to Library Skills Instruction," *School Library Media Quarterly* 13 (1985) 1:35–40.

———, "Inside the Search Process: Information Seeking from the User's Perspective," *Journal of the American Society of Information Science* 42, no. 5 (1991): 361-371.

———, "Implementing a Process Approach to Information Skills: A Study Identifying Indicators of Success in Library Media Programs," *School Library Media Quarterly* 22, no. 1 (1993): 11-18.

Loewenstein, G., "The Psychology of Curiosity: A Review and Reinterpretation," *Psychological Bulletin* 116, no. 1 (1994): 75-998.

Lumsden, Linda S., "Student Motivation to Learn," *ERIC Digest,* 92 (1994) (ED370 200).

Malone, Thomas W., and Mark R. Lepper, "Making Learning Fun: A Taxonomy of Intrinsic Motivations for Learning," *Aptitude, Learning, and Instruction, III. Conative and Affective Process Analysis,* edited by R. Snow and M. Farr (Hillsdale, NJ: Erlbaum, 1987): 223-253.

Maslow, Abraham H., "A Theory of Human Motivation," *Psychological Review* 50 (1943): 370-396.

McClelland, David C., *The Achieving Society* (New York: Free Press, 1961).

Miskel, C., J.A. DeFrain, and K.A. Wilcox, "A Test of Expectancy Work Motivation Theory in Educational Organizations," *Educational Administration Quarterly* 16, no. 1 (1980): 70-92.

Pappas, Marjorie L., and Ann E. Tepe, "Follett Information Skills Model," in *Teaching Electronic Information Skills* (McHenry, IL: Follett Software Company, 1995).

Plotnick, Eric, "Information Literacy," *ERIC Digest* (February 1999).

Rotter, J.B., "Generalized Expectancies for Internal Versus External Control of Reinforcement," *Psychological Monographs* 80 (1966): 69.

Seligman, Martin E.P., *Helplessness: On Depression, Development, and Death* (San Francisco: Freeman, 1975).

Small, Ruth V., "Motivational Strategies in Library and Information Skills Instruction: An Exploratory Study," *SLMR-Online* (Jan. 1999).

Small, Ruth V., and Marilyn P. Arnone, "Arousing and Sustaining Curiosity: Lessons from the ARCS Model," *Training Research Journal* 4 (1998): 103-116.

Stipek, Deborah J., *Motivation to Learn: From Theory to Practice,* 2d ed. (Boston: Allyn and Bacon, 1988).

Stripling, Barbara K., and Judy M. Pitts, *Brainstorms and Blueprints* (Englewood, CO: Libraries Unlimited, 1988).

Vroom, Victor H., *Work and Motivation* (New York: Wiley, 1964).

Weiner, Bernard., *Theories of Motivation: From Mechanism to Cognition* (Chicago: McNally, 1972).

Wilson, Brent G., ed., *Constructivist Learning Environments: Case Studies in Instructional Design* (Englewood Cliffs, NJ: Educational Technology Publications, 1996).

Wlodkowski, Raymond J., *Motivation and Teaching: A Practical Guide* (Washington, DC: National Education Association, 1984).

Yucht, Alice H., *Flip It! An Information Skills Strategy for Student Researchers* (Linworth Publishing, 1997).

Chapter Two

In the Beginning . . .

> **❝** It is the quality that moves us ahead, makes us more useful, even changes the world a bit. Without it we are condemned to be ordinary. With it we have a shot at being a part of the future. **❞**
>
> ~ S. Weintrub, 1986, p. 160

What do you think Weintrub was talking about? You'll find the answer later in this chapter.

Introduction

I n the beginning, there is ...

   ◆ Definition: an information need is specified.
   ◆ Selection: one or more potential topics are selected.
   ◆ Planning: information search strategies and potential information resources are
      considered.

In Chapter One, we reviewed the various information skills that students need
as they progress through the three broad stages of research. We also emphasized
the importance of understanding that students' attitudes and needs can influence
how they approach research tasks. We also discussed some of the key motivation
theories and concepts that will be used throughout this book. Finally, we presented
the Motivation Overlay for information skills instruction, which is intended to
provide guidance for the selection and use of various motivational techniques in your
information skills lessons.

In Chapter Two, we begin building a set of tools for incorporating those
concepts into motivational goals and techniques and offer examples of practical
strategies. By the end of Chapter Two you will:

   ◆ understand three key motivational goals related to the Beginning Stage of the
      research process, in which students define an information need and begin the
      process of selecting a topic and planning their information search strategies.
   ◆ begin to develop a repertoire of motivational techniques that can be used to
      address motivational goals in a given situation.

As stated earlier, this book assumes readers already have knowledge of and
some experience in teaching information skills and preparing related instructional
goals and objectives. We therefore focus on creating a set of motivation tools for
your lesson plans that integrates motivational goals in support of your instructional
goals. You can utilize these tools to enhance existing lessons, repair lessons that
didn't quite work the way you had intended, or create exciting new lessons.

Expectancy-value (E-V) theory is particularly relevant to the Beginning Stage of
the research process. Students must initially have the expectation that the research
task is both achievable and valuable before they will put forth the appropriate level
of effort to learn the skills they need. This means that students must have confidence
that they can acquire the requisite information skills and are capable of carrying out

the entire research process to a successful conclusion. They must also believe that learning the process and acquiring those skills are important and valuable.

Of course, E-V theory applies to adults as well, including the readers of this book! As a reader, you must expect that you can be successful in applying motivational concepts and that you see value in doing so. For that reason, we have incorporated the accounts of motivating teaching experiences contributed by a number of practitioners in the field. We hope, therefore, to build your confidence for implementing the ideas in this book through these real-life anecdotes (we call them "Motivational Moments") showcasing motivational techniques used by your colleagues and using the outcomes of their stories to reinforce the value of employing such techniques. We also sprinkle some of our own ideas throughout the chapters.

To help you accomplish the above motivational goals, we'll be building a "Motivation Toolkit" along the way. By the end of Chapter Two, your Motivation Toolkit will include a variety of techniques and some sample strategies for implementing these techniques during the Beginning Stage of research. Each technique and example strategy is connected to one or more motivation theories introduced in Chapter One.

What do we mean by techniques and strategies? We define techniques as the broad methods, activities, and approaches that support the motivational goals. One or more techniques may be used in meeting each goal based on a given situation or context. For example, one technique that is effective in generating interest and excitement (Goal #1) is to stimulate curiosity. Some ways by which this can be accomplished are posing an information problem, asking a question to launch a research project, and presenting a surprising fact or image that stimulates critical thinking about a topic.

Strategies are more specific and focus on means of implementing techniques. The following example uses specific strategies for implementing the broader technique, stimulating curiosity. The LMS collaborated with the seventh grade science teacher to introduce a lesson on researching national parks. She decorated the library media center with vacation paraphernalia, including a tent, a sleeping bag, and several colorful park posters, and dressed in a strange-looking hiking outfit. The teacher and LMS team-taught the lesson, discussing with students why some items of clothing might be useful and how others might be useless and even dangerous. The LMS asked students what information would be important to make these decisions and introduced them to a range of relevant information resources for finding weather-related and environmental information. The teacher and LMS used a creative way to stimulate curiosity for a topic that, if simply factually presented to students, might have seemed quite boring.

In many cases, the techniques described were inspired by problem situations; others were simply incorporated into lesson plans. The fact that LMSs often intuitively use motivational techniques in their library and information skills instruction was supported in a recent study conducted by one of the authors, who found that the information skills lessons taught by elementary and middle school LMSs consistently included a number of motivational strategies (Small, 1999).

As we present real-life situations (Motivational Moments) faced by educators from around the country (and the world), as well as our own experiences and ideas, we will frequently refer back to the theoretical foundation we provided in Chapter One and demonstrate where the various techniques fit within the Motivation Overlay. We hope we've set the stage for inspiring excitement about the motivational possibilities for your information skills curriculum. The figure on the next page shows the key motivational goals we will address for the Beginning Stage.

Figure 2-1. Motivational Goal #1: Beginning Stage

Research Stages	Beginning
Information Skills	Definition Selection Planning
Motivational Goals	✓ **Generate interest in the research process** Establish importance of information skills Build confidence in research ability
Related Motivational Theories	Expectancy-value Need Curiosity Attribution Social learning

We begin with Motivational Goal #1: **to generate student interest in the research process.** The motivational techniques we will discuss related to this goal are:

◆ creating positive anticipation for learning information skills

◆ stimulating curiosity for exploration and learning

We also describe a number of related strategies for inclusion in your information skills instruction.

Generating Interest in the Research Process

As we tackle the first important goal in the Beginning Stage of research, let's begin with a Motivational Moment from Tongay Epp on the next page, who found an interesting way to successfully address Goal #1 with a group of third graders.

▶ **Motivational Moment**

Library Media Specialist: **Tongay Epp**
School Name & Location: West Park Elementary School,
                            Columbus, Nebraska
Grade Level: 3
Instructional Goal: To analyze an information problem
Information Skill: Definition
Motivational Goal: To generate interest in the research
                            process

I believe it is important for the teacher and library media specialist to work together to clearly define the assignment. But rather than saying to the students, "We are going to study animals and you will need to find out its habitat, enemies, etc." we set up an information problem. In the world, we are given information problems to solve, not a list of things we should find out. So instead, the teacher and I planned together, decided on our learning objectives, and identified a problem that would lead students to learn what we had planned. For example, we gave the students this task: "You are an artist and have been contacted by city hall to set up an art exhibit on animal survival. Make an example of your artwork to give as part of an oral presentation to the city council members." Rather than our telling them, the students themselves had to think about the problem and decide exactly what information they needed to find. It works, the kids were quite excited about it, and it has application in real life. We also found that, through the creativity of the children, they often came up with some great ideas that we had never even thought of!

Tongay's Motivational Moment is an excellent example of Motivational Goal #1. She helped create positive anticipation for the research process by giving the students an authentic task (a real-life problem to solve) and letting them explore ways to solve it. The research project now had increased value to the students because they were directly involved in defining the parameters of the problem, constructing their own understanding of the problem, and creating one or more solutions.

Dale Lyles, a media/curriculum/technology specialist at Newnan Crossing Elementary in Newnan, Georgia, also endorses framing assignments as problems to solve, rather than what he calls a "search-and-destroy" report. Dale believes a problem-solving approach allows his students to more easily and accurately define their information needs. For example, Dale gave a group of fifth grade students the following challenge: "The King Tut exhibit was one of the biggest sensations in the museum world. Suppose our school was given the chance to get a portion of this exhibit to show in our library. Unfortunately, we would only be able to use a limited amount of physical space to show who King Tut was and why he was important. Your task is to design the exhibit."

Instead of creating their umpteenth written report, Dale's students became excitedly involved in such activities as creating floor plans, taking measurements, writing up placards, and designing a computer-based virtual-reality exhibit. Students who develop strategies for thinking through and solving problems demonstrate an ability to use information accurately and creatively (AASL and AECT, 1998). Dale's use of this type of problem-centered, project-based learning has been advocated by a number of prominent educational theorists, such as Howard Gardner (1991).

Returning to our first Motivational Moment, Tongay was also able to create a positive anticipation for learning by providing challenge and stimulating student interest in such a way that they must think in new and different ways. When researching what methods motivating teachers used, Wlodkowski (1990) cites providing challenge as one effective method.

Think back to Chapter One where McClelland's achievement motivation theory was discussed. In research on achievement motivation, researchers found providing challenges that are too difficult cause anxiety and frustration, while those that are too easy are boring and considered of little value. Both are demotivating. People high in need for achievement prefer learning tasks that are moderately challenging but attainable.

Tongay provided just the right level of difficulty for her students while still allowing them the freedom to be creative. It also sounds like Tongay was able to sustain their interest throughout the entire process by allowing the students the freedom to be creative about how they solved the problem. Furthermore, through Tongay's use of fantasy, she fired her students' imaginations and set up a learning environment conducive to flow (see Chapter One).

Here's an idea that might be especially effective with middle or high school students, particularly those who might not find research very exciting: sponsoring a "Student Researcher of the Month" award. Create a display in a prominent place so that students, teachers, administrators, and visitors can't miss seeing it. The display should include the student's picture, research topic, a synopsis of the project, and some interesting or surprising facts the student has discovered about his or her topic.

During her school library media internship, graduate student Renee Romance used some simple strategies to grab the students' interest and generate their excitement about research right from the beginning. She introduced the first lesson on resources for American presidents to eighth graders by playing "Hail to the Chief," asking students to identify the song, and then providing them with information on its origin. To introduce the second lesson for this unit, Renee read them a few humorous anecdotes she had found about Lyndon B. Johnson, demonstrating that not all of the information they discover as they do research will be dry facts, and that they may even encounter some humor (or mystery or novelty) along the way.

Here's an idea for creating positive anticipation for the research process that might be used with older students as they begin their research projects. Create posters and place them in strategic locations announcing that student researchers at your school would be featured in a local newspaper story. Once students have selected and narrowed their research topics, invite the education columnist from your local newspaper (or the editor of your school newspaper) to interview one or two students about what it is like to do research. It makes a great local human-interest story, provides excellent PR for your library and school, and underscores the value of research to students.

Jan Chemotti used an idea she found in *The School Librarian's Workshop* to generate an overall interest in the library as a supportive place that assists students in gaining access to rich resources and helpful services. Jan describes what she did in this next Motivational Moment.

▶ **Motivational Moment**

Library Media Specialist: **Jan Chemotti**
School Name & Location: West Genesee Middle School,
                            Camillus, New York

Grade Level: 6
Instructional Goal: To gain an awareness of the library media
                            center's resources, services, and staff
Information Skill: Planning
Motivational Goal: To generate interest in the research process

This was a finale to my sixth grade library orientation. Over three days students take a tour of the library, learn about the facility, learn about our procedures, about loan periods, discuss how important information is in their lives, meet the staff, explore our resources, and reinforce location skills in a kind of library "scavenger hunt." On the last day, I tell them that they're going to take a short library quiz. The "quiz" contains a short mystery story about their teacher being lost in the library. The story is missing information and students have to fill in the blanks with information they received during the library orientation. Every character in the story is one of the students in that class. I take each class list and word process the names of each student into the story. It takes a lot of time but the minute the students start realizing that their names are in the short story, they have a hilarious time with it and it really helps make the story and the information it contains memorable. Students who get a high mark on the quiz (and most of them do) receive "super" candy bars from me as a reward for being "super sleuths." The story reinforces the information that we think is really important—not only about loan periods or that you'll find a book about sharks in the nonfiction collection, but the names of my staff, the names of the library pets, etc. It also helps them realize that they're going to be held accountable for the information that they've received for the past three days, but we do it in a fun way so they develop an attitude that the library is a pleasant place to visit.

In addition to generating interest in what the library media center can do to help students be successful researchers, Jan accomplished several other goals in her Motivational Moment. By using students' names in her "quiz," she heightened their attention and made the orientation a relevant experience for each and every student. It is important, particularly at the beginning of the year, to establish rapport with students. Learning and using each student's name (and having students learn the names of the library staff) helps to do that. The students also gained an initial impression of the library media center as a supportive environment where they could confidently go for help with assignments and projects. This was an effective strategy for motivating these students to use the library in the future. Jan also provided unexpected rewards (candy bars) for student performance, which, in the short term, creates an incentive to work harder (Keller and Dodge, 1982).

Another technique for generating interest in the research process is to stimulate students' curiosity for exploring their world. We see this type of behavior in babies as they explore their environment by touching and tasting everything within their grasp. We see it in almost all preschoolers who pull things apart to explore what's inside (often to the chagrin of their parents). We also see it in young children who, when outside of the formal educational environment, seem "blessed with a seemingly limitless curiosity, a thirst for knowledge, a will to learn" (Lepper and Hodell, 1989, p. 73). What happens to these children, as we revisit them a few years later and discover they have become largely unengaged and disinterested, even in the most inherently interesting subject matter?

Stimulating curiosity is often a difficult challenge for educators; yet it is a critical element in motivating scholarship. Some researchers have found that while very young children are naturally curious about their environment and intrinsically motivated to learn, older children (from third to ninth grade) experience a decrease in intrinsic motivation and become more reliant on extrinsic motivators, such as grades, evaluative praise, and tangible rewards (e.g., Condry, 1978; Harter, 1981). This is, at least in part, due to factors in our educational system that constrain and routinize learning and suppress curiosity and exploration. Many attribute this decrease in curiosity to a progressive "decontextualization" of the curriculum (e.g., Condry, 1978), where content to be learned is presented according to a fixed schedule (a "just in case" approach), rather than at a time when students are ready and/or interested in learning it (a "just in time" approach).

Kuhlthau (1985) found that it is particularly important as students begin the research process that they be attentive and ask questions, as well as be open-minded to new ideas and information. All of these behaviors are associated with curiosity and interest. Diane Neary used a novel approach to stimulate curiosity and foster intrinsic motivation toward research when the fifth grade students visited her library media center.

▶ Motivational Moment

Library Media Specialist:	**Diane Neary**
School Name & Location:	Poly Prep Country Day School, Brooklyn, New York
Grade Level:	5
Instructional Goal:	To develop basic Internet search skills
Information Skills:	Definition, Selection
Motivational Goal:	To generate interest in the research process

Our school had just been wired for access to the Internet, using a T1 line. Many of the fifth grade students were new to the school as well as to the Internet. Providing an interesting way to introduce them to new resources is always at the top of my list as middle school library media specialist.

Collaborating with the fifth/sixth grade team of teachers, I learned about their plans to study the Iditarod dog race through science, geography, literature, and math. I added new books to the collection to provide daily race reports for their students but none of the classrooms was online. Using information from the teachers, I created and then mounted a website on several of the library's workstations to serve as a jumping-off place for fifth graders. Some of them were preparing to do research reports on different aspects of the race, and the more resources I could provide would help them in choosing and narrowing a topic. Our school's website had not yet been created, so I mounted this site as a "stand alone" in-house (i.e., in-library) site rather than waiting for the entire campus to be prepared for us.

Teachers allowed the fifth grade students to come to the library media center individually and in groups, whenever they possibly could. The students were anxious to check our "Iditarod/Ikidarod" website to find out their buddies' current standing. At the same time, they were developing a sense of comfort within the library media center, getting to know library personnel, and learning to look to them for help when needed. They were also learning basic Internet navigation skills and discovering that the Internet was one more information resource available in the school library media center.

While studying project-based learning, Blumenfeld et al. (1991) found that working on authentic, relatively long-term, problem-based projects builds students' intrinsic motivation, and one way to maximize motivational impact is to have students work with technologies, such as using computerized databases for conducting research. Combining the inherent appeal of computer technology with a meaningful research project almost guarantees motivated students. The library media center becomes the ideal environment for helping students explore their research topics using technology. As a result, Diane's motivational strategy accomplished several objectives. It stimulated her students' interest by using technology as an information resource that provided them access to information that (1) was the most up-to-date, (2) filled an information need that was important to them, and (3) was not accessible anywhere else. She also provided a means for acquainting students with the library media center and its staff and with the Internet in a way that created excitement and fun.

Diane's technique served to arouse her students' "epistemic curiosity" (a term introduced by Berlyne). Epistemic curiosity is a quest for knowledge, stimulated by an information gap that needs to be closed (Loewenstein, 1994). Diane's students' curiosity and interest centered on an ongoing need for the most current information on the status of the race.

Keller, in his ARCS Model of Motivational Design (1987), advocates using curiosity to help capture and maintain students' attention. Stimulating curiosity is a great way to help students develop an intrinsic motivation for knowledge seeking and lifelong learning. *Information Power* (AASL and AECT, 1998) suggests that the school library media specialist can be a powerful "catalyst" for motivating student curiosity and a spirit of inquiry that promotes lifelong, self-directed learning. By collaborating with classroom teachers to tie library and information skills to the students' classroom assignments and activities, Diane not only helped to stimulate students' curiosity but also provided a relevant context for learning that fostered ongoing intrinsic motivation.

The following anecdote from one of the authors provides another example of stimulating curiosity and a need to know. When she was an LMS in an urban elementary school, she worked closely with a group of sixth grade gifted (but often underachieving)

students. She decided to explore the topic of censorship with her students, using an innovative method. She shared with students a list of books that had been censored in one or more schools throughout the country and provided a shelf with several copies of each of the banned books on it. She then asked the students to select two books and determine why some people might try to keep others from reading them.

The students quickly became totally immersed in the exercise, and some time later one boy looked at his watch and exclaimed, "Wow! This is the first time I was working so hard I forgot about lunch!" It was true—they had all worked right through their lunch period. Students (and the LMS) had become so engrossed in the activity that they lost track of time and space. The flow phenomenon doesn't happen often, but when it does, it is a powerful motivator for learning and a memorable teaching experience. A learning environment conducive to flow combines curiosity, challenge, control, and reward simultaneously. In this example, the LMS provided an additional essential commodity, the time to become totally immersed in the activity. Kuhlthau acknowledges the importance of providing adequate time, particularly in the Beginning Stage of research.

Here's another strategy for stimulating students' curiosity you might want to try. Create a mystery box filled with fascinating questions on slips of paper to use as a starting point for helping students determine their research topics. Cover the mystery box with question marks and cut a hole in the top, just big enough for a student to be able to reach his or her hand in without being able to see into it. Place the mystery box prominently in the middle of the room where students cannot avoid seeing it as your lesson progresses, but don't acknowledge its presence. If students ask about it, tell them you can't reveal its contents yet. By the time you tell them what is in the box, your students will be squirming with excitement and curiosity. As each student pulls a question from the box, have him/her and the class brainstorm one or more topics and search strategies for exploring the answer to the question. If the student doesn't like the question, he/she can put it back and choose one more time. This is a great way to generate interest in exploring future information problems and research tasks and to give students an opportunity to practice their selection and planning skills.

Charlotte Poole, a K-8 LMS at Lakeshore School in Stevensville, Michigan, stimulates interest in classical literature with her seventh and eighth grade students by creating a "classic" environment. When the students arrive at the library media center, they are seated at tables set with placemats and napkins to give the whole room a more classic look. Each table has a bud vase with a single flower in it as a finishing touch. At this point, students' curiosity is piqued as Charlotte, dressed in black, serves "Classic Coke" and, with classical music playing in the background and a candelabra on the table near her, talks about classic books. She discusses the term "classic" and what it means with the students and has them think of other examples where classic is used, such as classic cars and classic films. It is easy to see why when Charlotte teaches this lesson, she says, "I have fun and so do they."

Charlotte uses the word "fun" to describe the experience for both herself and her students. Some people believe that if it's fun, students can't be learning, but we believe just the opposite. Anyone who has watched children at play knows that when it is fun, children are highly motivated. Making learning fun increases the likelihood that students will learn more and better. We even have an anecdote to illustrate this. As an LMS, one of the authors sat at a table with two children in the middle of the library media center. She had placed a stack of booklets containing the script of a charming and humorous play in the middle of the table and told them she had just received these plays and wanted to try them out. She and the two students took copies and began to assume roles and read the play. Because there were several parts, they started by taking two or three parts each. Pretty soon, another student wandered by and asked if she could join them. Then a boy who had come on a study hall pass overheard the laughter and asked to play one of the parts. Pretty soon there was a group of about eight students having a wonderful time reading the play, laughing, commenting on the plot, etc. As one student had to leave, another would join the group. And the best part of this story is that many of the students who voluntarily joined in and had the most fun were reluctant readers with a history of poor reading skills. The better readers helped them when they needed it but no one felt "on the spot" as they read. Kurt Hanks (1991) writes, "If you want to motivate people in any group, make their work fun!" (p. 37).

A curiosity-provoking strategy that Keller recommends is to create some sort of conceptual conflict that arouses a student's need to find information to resolve the conflict. Playing devil's advocate or introducing a startling or incongruous statement can do this. For example, one high school LMS we know collaborated with the health teacher on a research project exploring the effects of smoking on different parts of the body. When students entered the library media center to begin their projects, they encountered a large poster that said, "Smoking is good for you." This, of course, conflicted with students' existing knowledge and stimulated a vigorous debate for which students used a range of information resources to "disprove" this statement.

According to Wlodkowski and Jaynes (1990), there are three potential causes of learning boredom. The first is monotony—doing the same thing the same way over and over again. Small found that in her study as well, students often displayed off-task behaviors when the LMS continually used the same motivational strategies. The second cause of boredom is constraint, an overly structured environment in which there is a lack of freedom to learn and explore. The LMS can take advantage of an enriched learning environment that is highly conducive to information exploration and knowledge attainment. The third cause of boredom is the absence of a learning challenge, a topic we addressed earlier in this chapter.

Using a variety of motivational strategies that create positive anticipation and stimulate curiosity will go a long way toward preventing learning boredom. In a study that investigated which factors were considered by college students to be most important in avoiding and causing boredom, Small et al. (1996) found that students perceived their instructors as the primary source of learner interest and boredom. The factors students considered most likely to cause learning boredom were:

- a dry, monotone delivery style
- repetition of information students already knew
- irrelevant information
- a lack of variety of teaching methods

They also found that the most effective factors students named for *preventing* learning boredom were:

- ◆ opportunities for student participation and interaction
- ◆ relevant content
- ◆ humor
- ◆ instructor enthusiasm
- ◆ a variety of teaching methods

There is one thing to keep in mind, however, when planning strategies to arouse curiosity and interest. Some people are more comfortable than others with various curiosity-arousing situations and the level of stimulation they arouse. What is just the right amount of stimulation for one student might be too much or too little for another. Too much stimulation will generally result in students feeling overwhelmed and anxious, and any ambiguity in the research task will just compound the problem. Too little stimulation combined with an ambiguous research task will likely cause boredom. Either situation often results in withdrawal from the activity, sometimes permanently. This is consistent with what Kuhlthau found in her research.

Therefore, it is important to provide an environment that appropriately stimulates curiosity and an openness to new information and ideas. The curious student will want to explore and learn for learning's sake (see Small and Arnone [1998/1999] for a range of ideas for stimulating intellectual curiosity). Now you should know what Weintrub was talking about in the quote appearing at the beginning of this chapter.

Here is the first part of your Beginning Motivation Toolkit, designed to help you address Goal #1 of the Motivation Overlay. You will notice there are some unfilled spaces. As we build this Toolkit together, you can be thinking of new ideas or your own tried-and-true motivational strategies for customizing your Toolkit.

Figure 2-2. Motivation Toolkit Goal #1: Beginning Stage

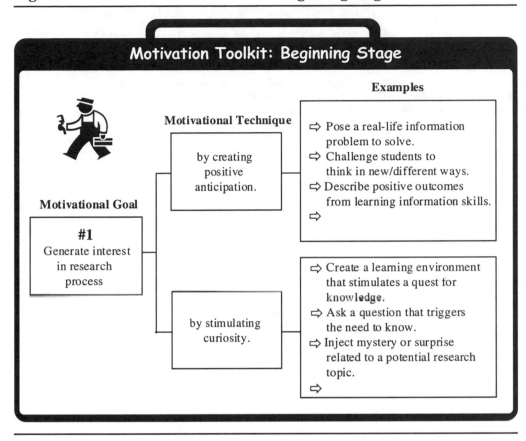

Before moving on to Motivational Goal #2, remember a necessary ingredient in the motivation mix—YOU! Your own enthusiasm in engaging in the research process and curiosity for learning will help to create positive anticipation and help your students see the research process as exciting. Most likely, you have chosen to be an LMS because you believe information literacy is a critical component of preparing students for learning success and success as future citizens in a democratic society. Thus, you are inspired to teach them the skills they need to be information literate. Use this inspiration to drive your outward enthusiasm. When students can connect to that enthusiasm, their motivation will increase. Best of all, enthusiasm is contagious; it will spread not only to your students but also to teachers, staff, administrators, and parents. It is the kind of modeling behavior advocated in Chapter One of this book.

Although we describe your enthusiasm as a necessary ingredient for creating a motivating information environment, it is by no means a sufficient one. So let's move on to Motivational Goal #2 in the Motivation Overlay: **to establish the importance of information skills**.

Figure 2-3. Motivational Goal #2: Beginning Stage

Research Stages	Beginning
Information Skills	Definition Selection Planning
Motivational Goals	Generate interest in the research process ✓ **Establish importance of information skills** Build confidence in research ability
Related Motivational Theories	Expectancy-value Need Curiosity Attribution Social learning

The techniques that we recommend for accomplishing Goal #2 are:

◆ building on existing knowledge and prior experience

◆ relating the research task to students' needs and interests

◆ describing the usefulness of learning information skills

We describe these techniques (and some strategies for implementing them) in more detail in the following section.

Establishing the Importance of Information Skills

Establishing the meaningfulness, relevance, value, or whatever synonym you wish to use can be accomplished in a number of ways. Eisenberg and Berkowitz (1990) advocate curriculum mapping, a systematic curriculum data collection/organization/presentation method that allows the LMS to identify and plan appropriate and relevant resources and services for the topics, assignments, and activities that teachers will cover throughout the school year at the time of need.

Methods like curriculum mapping reinforce the importance of teaching information skills in context, integrated with the curriculum.

Janice Wright used an innovative way to help her fifth grade students choose their research topics and formulate their research questions. In the following Motivational Moment, Janice describes a strategy that allowed her students to build on existing knowledge and prior experience.

▶ **Motivational Moment**

Library Media Specialist:	**Janice Wright**
School Name & Location:	Midlakes Intermediate School, Clifton Springs, New York
Grade Level:	5
Instructional Goal:	To prepare students for creating reports on the Civil War
Information Skills:	Definition, Selection, Planning
Motivational Goal:	To establish the importance of learning information skills

I was working with a fifth grade teacher on a unit about the Civil War following their recent field trip involving a reenactment they witnessed. In preparation for the students choosing their own topics and developing their own questions, I found a small article on prisons in the Civil War in our library's encyclopedia. I thought this might be of interest to most of them and not a topic any of them might think to pick.

The students were each given a copy of the article and I also made an overhead transparency. Before letting them read the article, I asked the students to turn the paper over and write down at least one or two questions they had about Civil War prisons. Next we recorded their questions and grouped them according to similar ideas. For example, many were about the prison building and the cells. Some were about the prisoners, number of them, their crimes, and punishments. After listing them all and grouping them, they turned their papers over and read the article, underlining all the answers they could find to their questions. It was great! They could see the importance of reading with their task questions clearly in mind. They could also see if this particular source would be helpful later for their reports, and which questions had not yet been answered.

The strategy that Janice used, building from the familiar to the new, is effective for motivating learning in general and works extremely well when applied to expanding a student's range and application of information skills. When one can link new learning to past knowledge or experience, it becomes more meaningful.

Here's one of our ideas for accomplishing this objective. When teaching students to use the Internet and World Wide Web as an information resource, start by having them describe ways they typically search for information using print sources. Display all of their ideas visually so the entire class can see them. Then put a big check mark in front of any idea that can also be used to search for information on the Web. In this way they discover they can transfer some of their tried-and-true searching methods to a new type of resource. Then use that as a springboard to teach the unique skills required for Internet and Web searching, such as Boolean logic. In this way, students can take what they already know and proceed to a new way of searching for information.

As students begin to formulate a research topic, Kuhlthau warns that they may harbor a number of preconceived ideas. Students need to be encouraged to be open-minded at this point in the process. Brainstorming is an excellent method for fostering creative problem solving and helping students broaden their perspectives and keep an open mind. Donham (1998) suggests that this method often results in more meaningful and fewer low-level, fact-based research questions. By having students brainstorm before looking at the article on Civil War prisons, Janice helped them maintain a degree of open-mindedness about their topic and discover how to generate innovative questions about a topic that they could explore beyond the information contained in any one article.

There was also another benefit to Janice's strategy. When students used group brainstorming to explore their questions, some of the apprehension that Kuhlthau describes as prevalent in the Beginning Stage of research decreased as students realized they already have skills that allow them to articulate many of the questions needed to be answered for their reports. Brainstorming is a safe, nonjudgmental method for trying out new and sometimes unconventional ideas.

Another strategy we find helpful for building on students' existing knowledge and experience is the concept map. Concept maps allow students to visually represent all of the information they know about a topic of interest.

A concept map is created by writing a main topic in a box drawn in the middle of an overhead transparency or piece of paper. Students are then asked to brainstorm related topics or ideas as the instructor writes them in boxes placed randomly around the center box. Lines are drawn connecting the main topic to each of the subtopics. Each subtopic may be related to a number of other subtopics. Relationships among subtopics may also be shown by drawing lines connecting them. We have created a concept map representing the various motivation theories and concepts and their relationships as described in this book. That concept map appears below.

Figure 2-4. Concept Map: Motivation Theories and Concepts

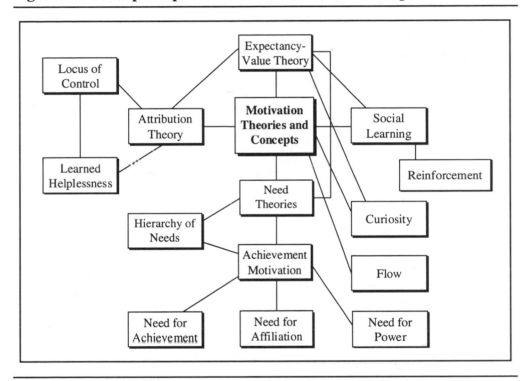

Describing the usefulness of information skills to the events in students' everyday lives is another excellent technique for establishing the importance of learning information skills. One simple way to do this is to have students list the decisions they make in a typical day (e.g., what clothes to wear, what cereal to have for breakfast, which friend to sit with on the school bus). Ask them to recount how they made these decisions and list the steps in their decision-making process. Then draw parallels to the process they will use to conduct research or solve information problems. An example of a similar activity for older students is having students plan what information-seeking strategies they could use to make a decision on how to spend their back-to-school clothing budget. Strategies might include searching through magazines for the latest trends, talking with peers, getting on the Internet and looking at websites designed specifically for their age group, reading ads in the newspapers, or visiting local stores and asking salespeople about the current best-selling items.

Ellen Rappaport helped her students discover how a familiar tool can sometimes be useful as a preliminary information source before formulating an information search strategy, as you will see in the following Motivational Moment.

▶ Motivational Moment

Library Media Specialist:	**Ellen D. Rappaport**
School Name & Location:	Barton Elementary School, Patchogue, New York
Grade Levels:	4 & 5
Instructional Goal:	To gain relevant strategies for evaluating and manipulating nonfiction materials
Information Skill:	Planning
Motivational Goal:	To establish the importance of learning information skills

I had all students bring their social studies textbooks to the library. Students were asked not to open the book. I asked the students to define the difference between fiction and nonfiction. The students all agreed nonfiction should be true. I then asked the students to tell me what subjects they felt they were very knowledgeable about; some said hockey, swimming, etc. I asked them if they were examining a book on one of these subjects, what would they want it to have. They began to create a list, which we displayed on the overhead projector. Some of the items on their list included actual photographs or drawings, captions, recent copyright, the person should be an expert (expert status would be gotten from credentials next to the author's name or a biographical sketch), bibliography, glossary, index, etc.

After this list was established, I asked the students to open their social studies books and look for these elements in their books. They were surprised and delighted to discover that their textbook had all of the important elements. I then asked the students if the same criteria would apply when they were examining a website or a CD-ROM product. The activity made them feel like "detectives" when approaching research tasks and heightened their awareness of the importance of closely examining factual materials in computer and print form for accuracy and point of view. They quickly agreed that these products should have the same requirements. I heard many students declare, as they left the library, "I'm taking my textbook home tonight!"

Students in the elementary grades need to learn how to evaluate nonfiction materials so that they can be effective researchers and efficiently locate accurate, current, and relevant information in various subject areas. Ellen's activity helped her students appreciate the relevance of a wide range of nonfiction information resources for helping them solve their information problems and called their attention to an old, familiar resource—their textbook. Through this activity they rediscovered their textbook as a potential information source for conducting research. What they learned about evaluating their textbook could then be applied to other information resources.

One idea we had for establishing the importance of learning information skills with primary grade students is to develop a special display or bulletin board for your school's Open House. This can be an excellent way for teaching early-level information search strategies. First, brainstorm with the class what the theme for the display will be. Once that is decided, tell them you want each of them to contribute something to the display and ask them how they will decide what to contribute. You might suggest they think of something related to the theme that their parents would enjoy and, through a guided brainstorming exercise, come up with a number of search strategies for finding this information (e.g., interviewing their parents, talking to their friend's parents, looking through library books). Generally, a school's Open House is of considerable importance to young students, and strategies like the above help them discover the usefulness of decision-making in a way that is meaningful to them. You'll see their excitement rise as they brainstorm possibilities for finding appropriate subject matter and ways to represent it.

Another method for pointing out the usefulness of information skills includes discussing how skills like defining, selecting, and planning might be of future value to students. This works particularly well with older students who already may be contemplating their careers. Have them suggest ways these skills are useful for a graphic artist, a construction worker, or an accountant.

Instruction that *relates to the needs and interests of students* helps establish the relevance of learning information skills. *Information Power* describes the information-literate student as an independent learner who "pursues information related to personal interests" (p. 23). Researchers have found that when students see personal interest or value in attaining knowledge, they will pay closer attention to the instruction, sustain it longer, and process the information taught at a deeper level (e.g., Brophy, 1998). We all know that there are some topics that consistently capture the imagination of students—information about which many students just can't seem to get enough (e.g., dinosaurs, rock music, science fiction, sports). Try using some of these personal favorites as subjects or keywords when teaching electronic search strategies. Or, have students write mini-research papers on a favorite topic and let them share their papers by putting them on a bulletin board or on the school's Web site. You will probably think of many other ways that you can incorporate the personal interests of students into research projects. You may now add Goal #2 to your Motivation Toolkit.

Figure 2-5. Motivation Toolkit Goal #2: Beginning Stage

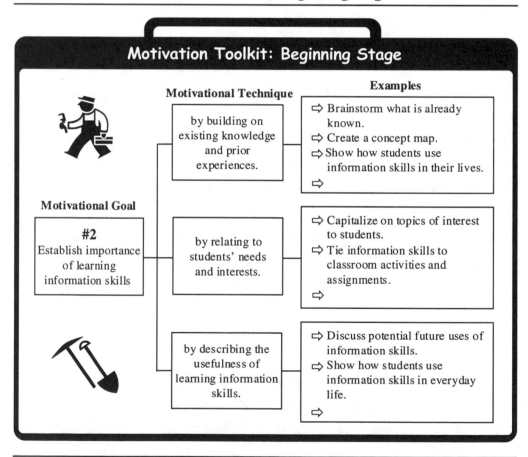

While establishing the importance of learning information skills is essential to the value aspect of E-V theory, helping students feel they are capable of learning information skills and completing research tasks is critical to having an expectancy for success. This is addressed in the Motivation Overlay's next motivational goal for the Beginning Stage of the research process: **to build student confidence in their research ability**.

Figure 2-6. Motivational Goal #3: Beginning Stage

Research Stages	Beginning
Information Skills	Definition Selection Planning
Motivational Goals	Generate interest in the research process Establish importance of information skills ✓ **Build confidence in research ability**
Related Motivational Theories	Expectancy-value Need Curiosity Attribution Social learning

We recommend three techniques for accomplishing this goal:
- ◆ offering a supportive learning environment for learning research skills
- ◆ providing an appropriate level of challenge in information skills instruction
- ◆ clarifying the requirements of the research task

The following section describes each of these techniques in more depth and offers several strategies for implementing them.

Building Confidence in Research Ability

Students begin to feel confident in their ability to learn and perform when they feel competent (i.e., they have the required skills and knowledge to succeed) and self-determined (i.e., they are in control of their learning). Kuhlthau (1985) found that there are several important factors directly related to building students' confidence in their research ability. In the Beginning Stage of the research process, when at least some apprehension and uncertainty may be expected to affect confidence, students (particularly inexperienced researchers) should:

◆ know what's expected of them

◆ have clearly defined parameters for the research task

◆ have a structured (but adequate) time frame within which to work

◆ receive reassurance and help in managing their feelings of uncertainty

◆ be encouraged to read and reflect

The LMS and classroom teacher can have a positive impact on all of these factors through the application of appropriate motivational strategies.

Another critical technique for helping students build confidence in their research abilities requires assessing each student's level of knowledge, skill, and research experience at the beginning of the information literacy instruction as part of our analysis of the learning audience. Only in this way can we confidently plan ways to individualize learning in order to *provide the appropriate level of challenge* to each student. Learning centers, individual learning packages, and other self-paced instructional delivery methods can help accomplish this.

The learning contract is another effective strategy for providing an appropriate level of challenge; in effect, it allows students to set their own learning challenges. A learning contract is a written agreement, typically between the instructor and each individual student, that specifies the type and extent of learning the student will achieve. Learning contracts have been heralded as helping students become more confident, self-motivated, and self-directed, allowing them to actively share control over what they will learn, how they will learn it, and how learning outcomes will be evaluated. As a result, students perceive their success or failure to be determined by their ability to accomplish the learning objectives they have set (Beare, 1986), fostering internal attribution and intrinsic motivation.

Providing a supportive learning environment is another method for building students' confidence in their ability to learn information skills and use them to complete research tasks. When these English teachers required a group of less-than-eager readers to select and read a work of British literature in order to fulfill an assignment, one LMS and her graduate student intern  worked together to design a lesson that helped make the task appealing to students while giving them the confidence that they could be successful. What they did is described in our next Motivational Moment, on the next page, by the intern who taught the lesson.

▶ Motivational Moment

Library Media Specialist: **Katherine Cronn**
Graduate Student Intern: **Jennifer Wielt**
School Name & Location: Oneida High School, Oneida, New York
Grade Level: 12
Instructional Goal: To read a work of British literature
Information Skills: Definition, Selection, Planning
Motivational Goal: To build confidence in students' research abilities

The LMS provided me with background information on the students. She knew that, although they are in Regents classes, a significant number of these students are not strong or eager readers. Most of them probably would come to the library with no clear idea of how to go about finding something to read, much less choosing something they would actually enjoy. Fortunately, the English teachers had a range of options for what was acceptable to read, from *Beowulf* all the way through current works. This gave them an element of control for the assignment, which I capitalized on in my lesson. And, because this was the first time the unit was being taught and because we had a limited time frame in which to work, they would have a limited selection of books to choose from.

So, I began the lesson by asking students to think of some ways they choose a book to read for pleasure, not a school assignment. Although a few students responded "I never read," many said, "I ask a friend to recommend something" or "I go in a store and read the backs of books" or "I choose something by an author I know I already like," which was exactly how I wanted them to think for this assignment. I also emphasized that their teachers, the LMS, and I could give them recommendations. I showed them the fiction section and pointed out that it was small enough for them to browse through. That way they could look for a book by an author they already knew and liked or could just read the jackets and other blurbs to see if they were interested. I tried to stress that the process of choosing a book didn't have to be any more complicated than choosing something for pleasure reading. I also gave mini-booktalks on several works of British literature, pulling in things I had read and enjoyed so that my enthusiasm would be apparent to students. I also demonstrated how to use several reference works for finding commentary on a work, information about a particular author, or a work on a specific theme in which they were interested. When I was done with the lesson, I asked students to repeat back to me all the ways they could use the library to find literature for their assignment, just to be sure they understood the process and as a reinforcement of my presentation.

Afterwards, I was pleased with the degree to which students responded to the task of finding a work of British literature to read for their assignment. Most of the works I described were chosen and many others as well. The best part was I noted a great deal of enthusiasm on their part for finding a "cool" or interesting book.

Jennifer used a number of motivational strategies to provide a supportive learning environment where her students could find success. She reinforced the control students could take over the assignment by reminding them they could use the same strategies for selecting a work of British literature as they do for selecting a book for recreational reading, which also provided relevance. She introduced students to the tools they could use to find out information about a book before reading it, to help ensure that it would be something they would enjoy. She assured students that the LMS, the classroom teacher, and she would be available for suggestions. She recommended some of her personal favorites with contagious enthusiasm, which gave them the confidence that these books were worthwhile and interesting. Finally, she had students repeat back to her what they had learned, which reinforced her confidence in them and their confidence in themselves.

The final technique for helping students feel confident about their research abilities is to *clarify learning requirements* at the beginning of instruction. This includes clearly articulating what students are expected to know by the end of the instruction, learning options that are available, and how and under what criteria their learning products will be evaluated. When students know exactly what is expected of them, they can begin to develop their competence as researchers and, with increasing confidence, become willing to take risks and try out new ideas.

Rubrics are an excellent method for precisely describing learning or performance standards. "Rubrics describe what learners should know and be able to do" (Spitzer et al., 1998, p. 144). Donham (1998) defines an assessment rubric as "an ordered set of criteria that clearly describes for the student and the teacher what the range of acceptable and unacceptable performance looks like" (p. 209). Since a rubric may be used as a guideline for excellence, students must have access to it before initiating the learning task. (For a detailed description of rubrics and how to create them for use in an information skills curriculum, see Donham, 1998, chap. 12.)

An LMS we know demonstrates the research process to her seventh graders by actually doing the assignment before the students do it. She completes the assigned worksheet on a topic of interest to her (in this case, hang gliding), telling students, "I decided to do this project myself to see what problems you might run into." This is a terrific strategy that allows the LMS to clarify learning requirements and expectations; determine any points of confusion students may encounter and plan ways to circumvent, decrease, or eliminate them; and model successful research skills and processes.

Susan Whittaker, a participant in one of our seminars, took away many ideas, some of which she used in the Motivation Moment on the next page. Susan used her creativity to plan a lesson to help a group of sixth grade girls increase their confidence in their ability to conduct research.

▶ Motivational Moment

Library Media Specialist:	**Susan Whittaker**
School Name & Location:	Whitney Point Middle School, Whitney Point, New York
Grade Level:	6
Instructional Goal:	To develop an informative display and induction speech for a Sports Hall of Fame
Information Skills:	Definition, Selection, Planning
Motivational Goal:	To build confidence in students' research abilities

Our sixth grade girls follow the Olympic Games with interest (especially the women's hockey team), as well as the increasing number of professional women's sports teams. However, enthusiasm and curiosity quickly fade with the idea of becoming a "sports historian." The research project is one of their first as middle schoolers. They believe the rumors about difficult middle school research papers, so I needed to find a way to change this expectation. They enjoy small group computer work and brainstorming activities, but these alone do little to build motivation when they feel uncertain about their ability to succeed in the middle school. These students may be curious about themselves and their peers, but they often lack enthusiasm for school activities. They doubt their own abilities to learn new information skills and see little value in the skills anyway. I want them to become intrinsically motivated, believing their efforts and abilities create success.

As originally designed, my lesson seemed to have few opportunities for success. Luck might help them find a useful site on their first search, but they probably will be unsuccessful in locating enough information in the two days allocated to complete their projects. This combination of factors creates an unmotivating learning situation.

So here's what I did. The whole idea of sports in the library is novel so I decided to build on that. When students arrived, I was dressed in a basketball jersey, swimming goggles, and ski boots and carried ice skates and a soccer ball, which immediately raised their curiosity as they tried to make sense of my appearance. I told the class I was trying to decide which was my favorite sport and surveyed the class for their favorites. I then asked students to estimate how many Olympic and professional sports were available for women when their mothers were their age and told them that they should ask their parents tonight for their estimates. Then, instead of calling on each student for answers, I asked students to call on each other to share ideas about what Olympic and professional sports women play today and record the responses on a brainstorming sheet I had provided. I explained that they would be nominating a woman into the Sports Hall of Fame, and passed out the assignment sheets clearly explaining the project and induction speech requirements in detail and providing a visual organizer for recording their research information. I then showed them the location of print resources on reserve and demonstrated where they could find relevant electronic resources. Both the teacher and LMS circulated to answer questions and offer guidance. The LMS provided special small group instruction during study hall periods to students who needed help. This way everyone was successful and enjoyed their first experience as middle school researchers.

Susan used a number of strategies to both clarify learning expectations and provide students with the support they needed to achieve. These strategies are highly effective for achieving Motivational Goal #3. Here are some others:

◆ Begin with a small step, clarifying the exact parameters of (and eliminating any misconceptions about) the assignment.

◆ Provide helpful hints when students get "stuck" and, whenever possible, be available for extra help if needed.

◆ Point out the generalizability of the information skills they are learning to other tasks and assignments.

All of these strategies are designed to help students develop an expectation for success. Although you alone can't erase years of failure and low self-esteem, you can have an impact on one area—developing the competence, skills, and confidence students need to be information-literate citizens.

Another strategy for helping students build confidence in their research abilities is to create lessons where students work in small groups, thereby sharing responsibility and providing learning support to each other. For example, the LMS could work with one or more elementary or middle school classroom teachers to connect a literature appreciation project with the annual school book fair. Students, working in small groups of three or four, could develop small group presentations on their favorite author. This is particularly appealing to students high in need for affiliation who derive satisfaction from working with others. With younger students or students with limited learning success, this type of group project helps increase their confidence as novice researchers. The LMS could have them define their task by asking them not only to choose their author but also to decide what their audience (other students, parents, teachers) would most want to know about each author (encourage them to think beyond typical information to find something unusual or funny to make their presentations more interesting). This increases the relevance of the assignment and makes it more fun.

Always make sure you set aside enough time for students to be able to use both print and electronic resources available in the library media center and that you are available to work with them if needed. Kuhlthau says that inexperienced researchers need a more structured time frame during the early stage of the

research process. As students enter the middle school grades and become more experienced, according to Wlodkowski and Jaynes, they can be allowed more flexibility and more control over structuring their learning experiences. The classroom teacher can help students prepare and rehearse their presentations. On the day of the book fair, students could be stationed near a display of a particular author's work and at specified times "present" their authors to book fair visitors.

Here is the final part of your Beginning Motivation Toolkit.

Figure 2-7. Motivation Toolkit Goal #3: Beginning Stage

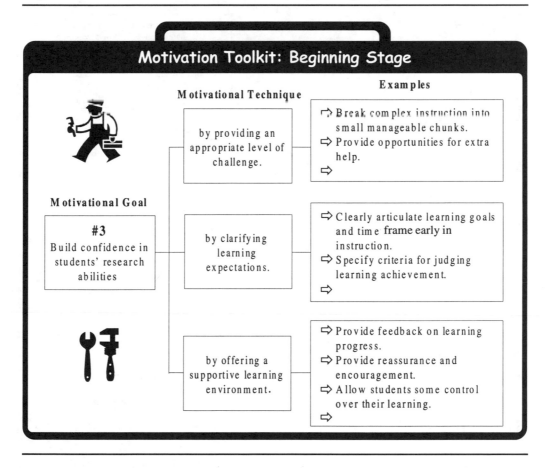

The entire Beginning Toolkit is on the next page.

Figure 2-8. Motivation Toolkit: Beginning Stage

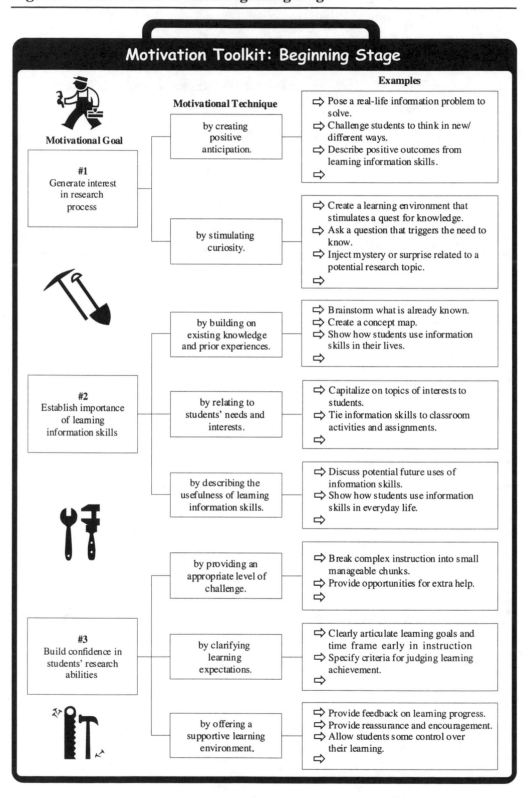

Throughout this chapter, we have focused on the first part of the Motivation Overlay, describing a variety of motivational techniques and strategies that you might want to consider incorporating into your information skills lessons during the Beginning Stage of research. Chapter Three focuses on ways to motivate students as they progress through the During Stage of research.

On the next page we present a "What Would YOU Do?" situation that allows you to contemplate a specific motivational challenge. We offer you one possible solution to the problem but encourage you to think of alternative ways of meeting the challenge.

What Would YOU Do?

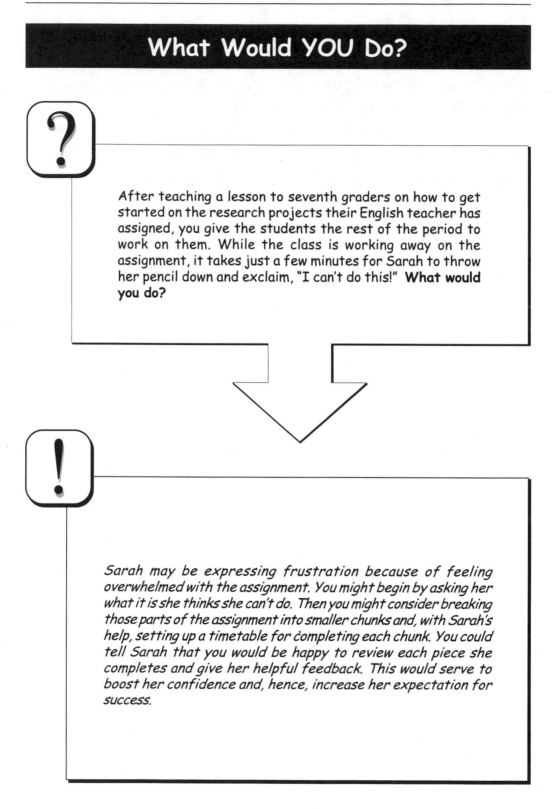

After teaching a lesson to seventh graders on how to get started on the research projects their English teacher has assigned, you give the students the rest of the period to work on them. While the class is working away on the assignment, it takes just a few minutes for Sarah to throw her pencil down and exclaim, "I can't do this!" **What would you do?**

Sarah may be expressing frustration because of feeling overwhelmed with the assignment. You might begin by asking her what it is she thinks she can't do. Then you might consider breaking those parts of the assignment into smaller chunks and, with Sarah's help, setting up a timetable for completing each chunk. You could tell Sarah that you would be happy to review each piece she completes and give her helpful feedback. This would serve to boost her confidence and, hence, increase her expectation for success.

Motivational Makeover

In this and the following three chapters, we include a "Motivational Makeover," a lackluster lesson plan that has been modified and expanded to incorporate a variety of motivational strategies. You'll notice that measures to assess the effectiveness of these strategies have also been included. Motivational Goals (as discussed in Chapter One) are not as precisely defined as instructional goals and objectives; you might even call them "fuzzy." Thus, measuring motivational effectiveness is also less rigid. Some methods for measuring student motivation are observation, self-report, increased student participation (such as asking questions), and, indirectly, amount and quality of student work.

Each of these Motivational Makeovers was submitted by a participant in one of our seminars. Thus, they had the benefit of recognizing just where their old lesson plans needed a boost and, because they had not yet been implemented, they are written in the future tense.

Our first example was submitted by Ann Gray of Pittsburg School, a K-12 school in Pittsburg, New Hampshire. Ann prepared this lesson for a group of highly motivated, activity-oriented sixth graders. It was their first major library research project. Unfortunately, the lesson fell flat. You'll find her Lackluster Lesson Plan on the next page.

▶ **Lackluster Lesson Plan**

Audience: Sixth graders

Topic: Ancient China and ancient India

Instructional Goal: To use different resources to find information about ancient China and ancient India and prepare a report

Information Skills: Definition, Selection, Collection, Presentation

Procedures:

1. Give the students the task.

2. Using one print and one electronic resource, students will prepare a report on both ancient China and ancient India.

3. A brief review of note-taking methods will precede the research.

4. Students will have three class periods to gather their information.

5. Students will turn in a two- to three-page typed report and their notes. The report must include citations in correct bibliographic format.

Ann analyzed the motivational problems with her lesson plan. Here are her thoughts.

"As I see it, there are several problems with the present lesson on ancient China and ancient India.

◆ There are no activities to get the students' attention and interest.

◆ Students have no choices available as to what information they will seek.

◆ No help is given to help students identify good resources to use.

◆ No guidance is given to help students clarify their learning task.

The audience is a group of sixth graders who are highly motivated and activity-oriented.

"They like being active and being able to move around. They tend to need to do short chunks of things at a time and to need attention-getting devices to maintain their interest. Also, this is the first major library research that they have done."

Ann thought about ways to motivationally improve her lesson to meet the needs of these students. As you examine Ann's Motivational Makeover, you'll note that improving the motivational quality of information skills lessons often requires expanding their scope and time frame in order to include more motivational techniques and strategies.

See if you can think of ways Ann might have spiced up her lackluster lesson. Then compare your ideas to what Ann suggests in her Motivational Makeover, which begins on the next page.

▶ Ann's Motivational Makeover

This instruction will be planned and carried out jointly with
the classroom teacher. The research portion time frame is
six or seven class periods on consecutive days. Two additional days will
be allocated for preparation for the Cultural Festival.

Audience: Sixth graders

Topic: Ancient China and ancient India

Instructional Goals: To create a better understanding of life in ancient
China and ancient India. To gain some introductory experience with the
research process.

Information Skills: Definition, Selection, Planning, Exploration, Collection,
Organization, Presentation, Evaluation

Motivational Goals: To generate interest in the research process. To build
confidence in research ability.

Motivational Measures: Demonstrations of student enthusiasm for the
research process. Improved quality of the students' work.

Lesson Plan:

1. As the students enter the library, they will see posters from India and
    China displayed.

2. Rather than have everyone in the class research both ancient China
    and ancient India, the class will be divided in half, with half doing
    ancient China and half doing ancient India.

3. In order to give the students more choice in what information they
    will find, they will be provided with a sheet that outlines six tasks,
    corresponding to each of Bloom's Taxonomy levels. Each task will have
    two choices under them and the students will choose one from each.
    This will also help to provide clear task definition. In order to generate
    some interest, these sheets will be decorated with graphics from
    ancient China and ancient India.

4. Students will be provided with worksheets on which they will fill in
    the information they have found for each of the choices they've made
    from the six tasks. At the top of the worksheet, they will be asked to
    define what their task is so that the LMS can clarify any problems
    before they get into the process too far. In addition, it will provide
    space for each student to write down the recipe that they have found.
    This will help students stay on task and provide them with a checklist
    for keeping track of their progress.

continued on next page

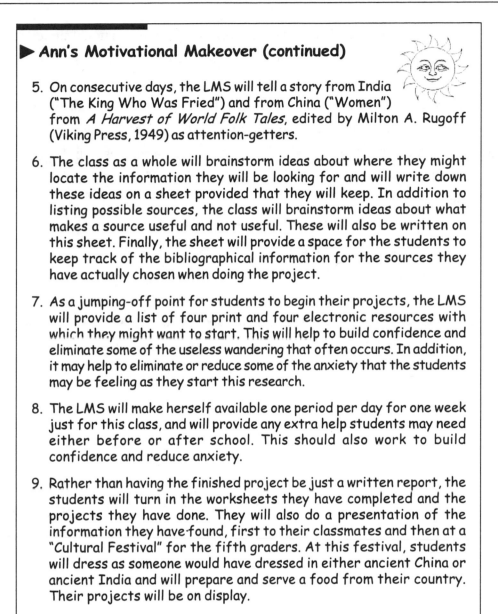

▶ Ann's Motivational Makeover (continued)

5. On consecutive days, the LMS will tell a story from India ("The King Who Was Fried") and from China ("Women") from *A Harvest of World Folk Tales*, edited by Milton A. Rugoff (Viking Press, 1949) as attention-getters.

6. The class as a whole will brainstorm ideas about where they might locate the information they will be looking for and will write down these ideas on a sheet provided that they will keep. In addition to listing possible sources, the class will brainstorm ideas about what makes a source useful and not useful. These will also be written on this sheet. Finally, the sheet will provide a space for the students to keep track of the bibliographical information for the sources they have actually chosen when doing the project.

7. As a jumping-off point for students to begin their projects, the LMS will provide a list of four print and four electronic resources with which they might want to start. This will help to build confidence and eliminate some of the useless wandering that often occurs. In addition, it may help to eliminate or reduce some of the anxiety that the students may be feeling as they start this research.

8. The LMS will make herself available one period per day for one week just for this class, and will provide any extra help students may need either before or after school. This should also work to build confidence and reduce anxiety.

9. Rather than having the finished project be just a written report, the students will turn in the worksheets they have completed and the projects they have done. They will also do a presentation of the information they have found, first to their classmates and then at a "Cultural Festival" for the fifth graders. At this festival, students will dress as someone would have dressed in either ancient China or ancient India and will prepare and serve a food from their country. Their projects will be on display.

10. Students will fill out an evaluation sheet after the festival, which will help them to evaluate their research skills and some of what they have learned. This will help build their confidence for the next time they must complete a research project.

Ann's Motivational Makeover is chock-full of great motivational strategies. For example, she uses posters to stimulate curiosity. She also puts graphics on worksheets to make them more interesting.

The worksheets help students keep track of their progress, thus enhancing their confidence in their ability to complete the research task. She uses additional confidence-builders, such as providing a list of potential resources at the beginning, being available for extra help throughout, and requiring self-evaluation after the Cultural Festival.

Ann also provides students with choices about the tasks they will be doing, thus increasing their relevance. This also helps students assume responsibility for their own learning. She uses a number of attention-getting strategies, including storytelling, brainstorming, and the Cultural Festival.

Ann has been pretty thorough in thinking about how to make research more exciting for her students. Can you think of other ways in which you might have improved her lesson for the students with whom you work?

▶ Chapter Challenge

Now that your Motivation Toolkit is filled with ideas for motivating students at the Beginning Stage of research, you are ready to accept the Chapter Challenge! Here are some questions to help you review some of the key ideas covered in Chapter Two. You can check your answers against ours on the next page.

1. Why is expectancy-value theory particularly relevant at the Beginning Stage of the research process?

2. What, according to Wlodkowski and Jaynes, are three potential causes of learning boredom?

3. What type of learning task do people high in need for achievement prefer?

4. In what grade does research indicate there is evidence of the beginning of a decline in natural curiosity?

5. What type of curiosity stimulates a quest for knowledge?

6. What method, developed by Eisenberg and Berkowitz, may be used to gather information for providing relevant information resources and services?

7. What feelings do students often experience early in the research process, according to Kuhlthau?

8. What motivational technique is especially important for building the confidence of lower-ability students?

9. Modeling enthusiasm for the research process is an example of what motivational theory?

10. According to Kuhlthau, what is it important to provide inexperienced researchers during the early stage of the research process?

▶ **Chapter Challenge: Answers**

1. Students must initially have the expectation that the research task is both achievable and valuable before they will make the effort to learn information skills.

2. Monotony, constraint, and lack of challenge.

3. Moderate but attainable challenge.

4. Third grade.

5. Epistemic curiosity.

6. Curriculum mapping.

7. Anxiety and feeling overwhelmed.

8. Providing a supportive learning environment.

9. Social learning theory.

10. A structured time frame.

Reflection Points

Please use this page to record your ideas and the special points you wish to remember from Chapter Two.

References

AASL and AECT, *Information Power: Building Partnerships for Learning* (Chicago: American Library Association, 1998).

Beare, Patricia G., *The Contract—An Individualized Approach to Competency-Based Learning and Evaluation* (Syracuse, NY: ERIC Clearinghouse on Information & Technology [ED 276 437] 1986).

Berlyne, Daniel. E., *Conflict, Arousal, and Curiosity* (New York: McGraw-Hill Book Company, 1960).

Blumenfeld, P., E. Soloway, R. Marx, J. Karjcik, M. Guzdial, and A. Palinscsar, "Motivating Project-based Learning: Sustaining the Doing, Supporting the Learning," *Educational Psychologist* 26 (1991): 369-398.

Brophy, Jere, *Motivating Students to Learn* (Boston: McGraw-Hill, 1998).

Condry, J., "The Role of Incentives in Socialization," *The Hidden Costs of Reward* (Hillsdale, NJ: Erlbaum, 1978), 179-192.

Donham, Jean, *Enhancing Teaching and Learning: A Leadership Guide for School Library Media Specialists* (New York: Neal-Schuman Publishers, 1998).

Eisenberg, Michael E., and Robert E. Berkowitz, *Information Problem-Solving: The Big Six Skills Approach to Library and Information Skills Instruction* (Norwood, NJ: Ablex, 1990).

Gardner, Howard, *The Unschooled Mind: How Children Think and How Schools Should Teach* (New York: Basic Books, 1991).

Hanks, Kurt, *Motivating People: How to Motivate Others to Do What You Want and Thank You for the Opportunity* (Menlo Park, CA: Crisp Publications, 1991).

Harter, Susan, "A New Self-Report Scale of Intrinsic Versus Extrinsic Orientation in the Classroom: Motivational and Informational Components," *Developmental Psychology* 17 (1981): 300-312.

Kehoe, Louise, "Lost in the Library: A Middle School Orientation," *The School Librarian's Workshop* (Sep. 1993): 7.

Keller, John M., "The Systematic Process of Motivational Design," *Performance & Instruction* (1987): 1-8.

Keller, John M., and Bernard Dodge, "The ARCS Model of Motivational Strategies for Course Designers and Developers" (Fort Monroe, VA: Training Developments Institute, Sep. 1982).

Kopp, Thomas W., "Designing Boredom out of Instruction," *Performance and Instruction* 21, no. 4 (1982): 23-27, 32.

Kuhlthau, Carol, *Teaching the Library Research Process* (West Nyack, NY: The Center for Applied Research in Education,1985).

———, "Inside the Search Process: Information Seeking from the User's Perspective," *Journal of the American Society of Information Science* 42, no. 5 (1991): 361-371.

———, "Implementing a Process Approach to Information Skills: A Study Identifying Indicators of Success in Library Media Programs," *School Library Media Quarterly* 22, no. 1 (1993): 11-18.

Lepper, M.R., and Melinda Hodell, "Intrinsic Motivation in the Classroom," *Research on Motivation in Education: Goals & Cognitions*, vol. 3 (San Diego: Academic Press, 1989), 73-105.

Loewenstein, G., "The Psychology of Curiosity: A Review and Reinterpretation," *Psychological Bulletin* 116, no. 1 (1994): 75-998.

McClelland, David C., *The Achieving Society* (New York: Free Press, 1961).

Small, Ruth V., "Motivational Strategies in Library and Information Skills Instruction: An Exploratory Study," *School Library Media Research* <www.ala.org/aasl> (Jan. 1999).

Small, R.V., and M.P. Arnone, "Arousing and Sustaining Curiosity: Lessons from the ARCS Model," *Training Research Journal* 4 (1998/1999):103-116.

Small, R.V., B.M. Dodge, and X. Jiang, (1996). "Student Perceptions of Boring and Interesting Instruction," in *Proceedings of the Annual Conference of the Association for Educational Communications and Technology*, Indianapolis, Feb. 1996.

Spitzer, Kathleen L., Michael B. Eisenberg, and Carrie A. Lowe., "Information Literacy: Essential Skills for the Information Age" (Syracuse, NY: ERIC Clearinghouse on Information & Technology, 1998).

Weintrub, S., "Curiosity and Motivation in Scholarship," *The Journal of General Education* 38, no. 3 (1986): 159-166.

Wlodkowski, Raymond J., "Encouraging Motivation for Continuing Adult Learning," *Enhancing Adult Motivation to Learn.* (San Francisco: Jossey-Bass, 1990).

Wlodkowski, Raymond J. and Judith H. Jaynes., "Overcoming Boredom and Indifference," *Eager to Learn.* (San Francisco: Jossey-Bass, 1990).

Chapter Three

. . . During the Research Process . . .

66 I have always had a fancy that learning might be made a play and a recreation to children; and that they might be brought to a *desire* to be taught, if only learning were proposed to them as a thing of delight and recreation, and not a business or a task. 99

~ John Locke, 1693, Part IX, Section 148

Introduction

It is fascinating to think that over 300 years ago, scholars like John Locke had already recognized the importance of motivation for learning. In Chapter Two we presented the first part of the Motivation Overlay for Information Skills Instruction, which identified the information skills, motivational goals, and related theories for instruction at the Beginning Stage of the research process. Now let's explore some motivational techniques for the During Stage of the research process and continue to develop a practical, useful Motivation Toolkit for you to use in your information literacy instruction.

Once we have gotten students excited about beginning the research process, our challenge becomes keeping them motivated *throughout* the process. As students begin to explore information, they continue to feel that high level of anxiety that Kuhlthau describes in her research. For many students (even those who are already secure with their topic), as they wade through the voluminous amounts of information available to them, they may begin to change their topic, they may become overwhelmed with the number of potential topics, or they may not know how to narrow their area of research from a general to a specific topic. As a result, this is a time when the level of student confusion heightens, interest dips, and the need for a supportive learning environment intensifies. Once they have settled on a topic and the topic is of manageable breadth, Kuhlthau (1991) states that their feelings of uncertainty and anxiety give way to a sense of optimism, and subsequent collection and organization activities become less stressful.

In this chapter, we continue to build our Motivation Toolkit, exploring ways to sustain our students' motivation. By the end of Chapter Three, you will:

◆ understand three key motivational goals related to the During Stage of research in which students learn to explore, collect, and organize information

◆ be able to suggest a variety of motivational techniques that can be used to address motivational goals in a given situation during the research process

In the During Stage of the research process, there is:

◆ **Exploration:** specific sources are accessed and explored and the research topic is finalized.

◆ **Collection**: relevant information is gathered from various sources.

◆ **Organization:** information is summarized, sequenced, and synthesized.

The three key motivational goals for the During Stage of research, shown in the figure below, are critical for maintaining and sustaining student motivation during the research process. As we go through each of them and continue to build our Motivation Toolkit with motivational techniques and example strategies for achieving the key goals, think about ways to use or adapt our suggestions or develop original ones to implement with your students.

We now proceed with the next part of the Motivation Overlay, beginning with Motivational Goal #1 of the During Stage: **to maintain interest in the research process**.

Figure 3-1. Motivational Goal #1: During Stage

Research Stages	During
Information Skills	Exploration Collection Organization
Motivational Goals	✓ **Maintain interest in the research process** Promote value of information skills Reinforce confidence in research ability
Related Motivational Theories	Expectancy-value Need Flow Attribution Social learning

---

We present two techniques for accomplishing this goal. They are:

◆ providing variety

◆ promoting inquiry

For each of these techniques we describe a number of motivational strategies for implementing them.

Maintaining Interest in the Research Process

An old saying suggests that "variety is the spice of life." Variety may also spice up your information skills lessons and prevent learning boredom. ***Providing variety*** also accommodates the different learning styles students bring to the learning experience. We often teach the way we learn rather than the ways our students prefer to learn. Recognition of the range of learning styles that exist within any group frees us to use this information about learning styles "as a framework to describe the cognitive and affective diversity of students and, in turn, promote a diversity of instructional methods to support and enhance variations among students" (Davidson, 1990, p. 38). For example, some students prefer to learn individually and others in groups. Some learn best when presented with visual information such as pictures or flowcharts, others prefer verbal (oral) information, while still others want information in written form. Some students learn most effectively when an overview precedes the presentation of the content while others prefer a summary after the content has been presented.

Some ways to provide variety in information skills instruction are to:

◆ use a variety of teaching techniques (such as mini-lectures, discussions, brainstorming, role-playing)

◆ vary your voice to emphasize important concepts and change the pace of the instruction

◆ vary the media (such as videos, computer software, print handouts, posters) used to supplement instruction

◆ use various student grouping methods (such as individualized learning centers, small cooperative group projects, large group activities)

Varying specific instructional strategies within a lesson can also help to maintain student interest. Here are some ideas:

◆ While describing each of the search tools students will use, you can display visuals that represent concepts or skills to be learned. For example, one LMS we know uses a giant poster of a very real-looking pizza cut in large pieces, each piece labeled to represent each of the steps in the research model she teaches her students. She picks up each slice of pizza, describes its step in the process, and gives several examples. She then issues a "pizza challenge" to each class. Every time a student in the class uses one of the information skills in the pizza, the class gets a point. The class with the most points wins a pizza party. The pizza image makes learning the process unforgettable and the challenge makes learning a lot more exciting.

◆ Use memory enhancement techniques to help students remember the steps in the research process as they work through their projects. For example, work with students to develop mnemonic devices for important content. Remember ROY G BIV (the colors of the rainbow in order)? How many of us still have to mentally recite the rhyme "Thirty days have September, April, June, and November" to remember the number of days in a particular month? Anyone who has learned to read music knows FACE and Every Good Boy Does Fine (EGBDF), mnemonics to remember the notes on the spaces and lines. Mnemonics are both fun to create and useful. One LMS developed the mnemonic "TILUSE" to help her students remember the steps in the Big Six (each letter stands for each of the steps in the process) and repeats the sentence, "*Till* you *use* this, you don't get good information."

◆ Sprinkle instructional materials with humor, where appropriate. For example, add some relevant cartoons to instructional materials to make them more interesting and fun.

◆ Allow students to choose from a variety of ways to present the product of their research. This idea will be discussed in more detail in Chapter Four.

◆ Require students to gather relevant information from a variety of sources (print, electronic, human).

◆ Inject cueing statements that alert students to important information (e.g., "This is particularly important" or "Pay close attention here").

In the Motivational Moment on the next page, Jan Ziglin and her colleagues adapted a personal narrative writing idea from the I-Search process (Make It Happen Program) to "cook up" her information skills lesson. I-Search is a research reporting technique in which students write about their topic in the first person. (For more information about the I-Search process, see Joyce and Tallman, 1997.)

▶ **Motivational Moment**

Library Media Specialist: **Janice Ziglin**
School Name & Location: Pilgrim Park Middle School,
                            Elm Grove, Wisconsin
Grade Level: 8
Instructional Goal: To complete a research report on China
Information Skills: Exploration, Collection
Motivational Goal: To maintain interest in the research process

An eighth grade social studies teacher, English teacher, reading teacher, and I collaborated on an I-Search project we developed on a study of China. It was fabulous and very rewarding. Part of our goal was to encourage the students to use all kinds of resources, from the reference books I taught them about to interviews with people they might know who knew something about their topic. The teacher developed a list of possible topics from which the students could choose. They kept track of the process as they went along, writing sections of their final report. One section detailed their search for information. For example, one student wrote, "I first looked in the World Book Encyclopedia to get an overview of foods in China. Then I found a cookbook with much information in our school library and I took notes from that. Then I went to the public library with my friend and we found three books that were very helpful with recipes. Finally, we visited a local Chinese restaurant and interviewed one of the cooks." The students turned in a written report and also had to give a visual presentation of some sort to the class. In the example above, the student videotaped the cook at the Chinese restaurant preparing a dish.

Janice's Motivational Moment reinforced the *value* of using a variety of information resources to complete a research project. It helped students be aware of different perspectives and approaches to the same topic and made the topic much more interesting. The personal narratives required students to reflect on the process as they were going through it, rather than waiting until the end. Strategies like the ones Janice used not only can generate student excitement but also can rejuvenate the LMS's creativity and enthusiasm. (For more information on the I-Search personal narrative, see Macrorie [1988] and Joyce and Tallman [1997].)

The importance of variety is greater the younger the students; elementary students need more physical movement and sensory stimulation than high school students. But all learners (even adults) need some variety in the way information is organized and presented to them.

Kendra Sikop, an LMS from Longmeadow, Massachusetts, and a participant in one of our seminars, took a lesson plan she found about bears in *School Library Media Activities Monthly* and redesigned it, motivationally speaking. She thought the lesson plan was trying to accomplish too much in one lesson, especially with seccond graders, so she broke it up into several separate, but related, lessons that comprise an interdisciplinary math/science unit on bears. Since the students have an overall positive attitude toward learning, her lesson plan focuses on *maintaining* their curiosity and interest in researching information, mainly through a variety of activities and resources. Because it is still a plan (Kendra hasn't had a chance to implement it yet), it does not yet qualify as a Motivational Moment and we describe it using the future tense.

In Kendra's plan, the LMS and classroom teacher will collaborate to teach the students to understand and recognize the concepts of compare and contrast and to relate this understanding to mathematical units of measure. When the students come to the library media center, they will use specific sources to collect weight and size information on three different bear species (polar, black, brown). They will then transfer their findings onto an electronic spreadsheet to be presented to the class. Kendra's school is technologically progressive, so students have been exposed to using technology on a regular basis since kindergarten. Here's how Kendra describes the lesson:

"The environment of the school media center is organized creatively to attract student attention, help orient and focus students on the given task, work in teams, and make the process an enjoyable, positive, and engaging experience for the entire class. In addition, since the average class size is 20-25 students, this lesson will have half the class at a time come to the school media center. This will ensure less disruption and more immediate feedback from the LMS.

"Bear paw prints will lead the students from the classroom to the school media center. Three information resource stations will be set up in the library media center: Boris Black Bear from Russia (Station 1), Pia Polar Bear from Alaska (Station 2), and Benjamin Brown Bear from Massachusetts (Station 3). In teams of three, children will visit each station to work cooperatively to find height and weight, geographic, and habitat information. Each station will contain a computer where children can access information using the CD-ROM encyclopedia and a couple of preselected print resources. Teams will complete a predesigned chart, which will help students organize their information according to how they will transfer it onto an electronic spreadsheet in a future lesson. The LMS and aide will circulate among all three stations to provide feedback, praise, and encouragement.

"At the same time, the other half of the class and the teacher will be in the media center classroom to hear information from and ask questions of a visiting zoologist (who also cares for bears at the local zoo) concerning why conducting research on bears is important. Once each half of the class completes their activity, they switch.

"After all students have completed both activities, the students will gather as one group in the library media center where there is a scale and a large poster on the wall showing a life-size outline of an adult female polar bear. The teacher and LMS will ask students: 'How many of you make up the weight of one adult male black bear?' (several students will weigh themselves and form a group until they have reached the appropriate weight) and 'How does your height compare with a female adult polar bear?' (students can stand next to the drawing to make comparisons)."

Kendra incorporates many motivational strategies into her lesson. The paw prints stimulate students' curiosity in what they will find once they reach the media center. Using different bear themes for each learning center makes the learning more fun and breaks the learning about each type of bear down into a manageable learning chunk. By dividing the class in half, Kendra ensures that students will receive individual attention and enjoy a more comfortable environment, particularly for those who might be too shy to ask questions in the larger group. By letting students work in small groups, she also accommodates the need for affiliation.

Students are able to access a variety of information sources (electronic and print) to gather information. The preselected sources, predesigned chart for recording their information, and the individual guidance, feedback, and encouragement from the LMS and aide will help to increase students' confidence and expectation for success.

The meeting with the zoologist reinforces the value of the learning task. Finally, the height and weight activities at the end of the lesson continue to raise students' epistemic curiosity. Watch their eyes widen as the number of students needed to equal the weight of one male black bear builds and as each student stands next to the poster of the female polar bear in order to compare heights. Kendra would also like to find a way to "adopt" a baby bear from a local zoo or through the Internet to allow students to monitor the weight and height developments of the bear throughout the school year, thereby continuing to stimulate their interest and curiosity and allowing students to use technology in an innovative way.

Introducing new sources and unusual types of information during the research process, while possibly contributing to some of what Kuhlthau (1985) calls "technical uncertainty" (i.e., uncertainty about how to use databases and other information resources), can also help to sustain the curiosity you piqued in students in the Beginning Stage and increase their perception of the importance of continuing the information search. In the Motivational Moment on the next page, Mary Alice Brunell does just that by using multimedia technology to introduce a group of fourth graders to some fascinating information about explorers.

▶ **Motivational Moment**

Library Media Specialist:	**Mary Alice Brunell**
School:	Charles E. Riley Elementary School, Oswego, New York
Grade Level:	4
Instructional Goal:	To research information about explorers to the New World
Information Skill:	Collection
Motivational Goal:	To maintain interest in the research process

The New York State Social Studies curriculum introduces fourth graders to the explorers of the New World. One fourth grade class came to the library to research facts about a particular explorer. They were accustomed to searching through print resources to find the information they needed so I decided to introduce the Internet as a potential information source. I bookmarked a site on the Internet that allowed students to explore links relating to their explorer. Using an LCD panel to project my search to the entire class, I demonstrated how to access this bookmarked site and how to link to sites about their explorer. The students were so interested to see maps, illustrations, paintings, and essays that held the information that they were looking for. The room was just "a-buzz" with excitement as students announced some of the unusual and interesting facts that they had discovered. The variety of information and the multimedia format truly held the students' attention and interest.

Mary Alice's students learned they could access a variety of types of information about a single topic at one time on the Web. This helped stimulate their interest and continuing curiosity about their topic.

"Tell me, I forget. Show me, I remember. Involve me, I understand." This ancient proverb wisely reminds us that we learn best when we are active participants in the learning process, rather than passive recipients of information. *Promoting inquiry* through questioning is an excellent technique for encouraging participation and maintaining student interest in the research process.

Inquiry can be promoted in two ways. First, you can *encourage the students to ask questions* at various points in the research process, particularly at times when you know they may be anxious, confused, or frustrated. This is a good way of promoting participation. Furthermore, your answers may calm any worries or fears they might have. Sometimes just seeing that other students also have questions (and even the same ones as yours) can be comforting.

Another method for maintaining interest in the research process is by *posing questions to students*. For example, you could ask a provocative question about a research topic, such as "What might have happened if ...?" or an open-ended question such as "What plan can you develop for solving ...?" Posing questions that go beyond factual information and require students to use higher-level thinking skills, such as analysis, synthesis, and evaluation, can generate lively discussions and a newfound excitement in exploring information.

It is also important to remember, when asking students higher-order questions, to provide adequate time for responding. Often we don't give students enough time to think about the question asked and formulate an answer. Rowe (1986) calls this "wait time." As Rowe found, simply by waiting three to five seconds after asking a question of students, you will likely have many more students responding, their responses will be of higher quality, and they will be more apt to continue participating.

Have you ever tried waiting for three to five seconds? Take a stopwatch and wait five seconds in a quiet room. Even this very short length of time can seem like an eternity during silence. But don't worry about the silence; it probably means your students are thinking about your question and working on an answer. The next time you ask students a question, slowly count to five in your head. We think you'll be surprised and pleased with the results.

On the following page is the next part of your Motivation Toolkit, containing techniques and potential strategies for maintaining students' interest in the research process.

Figure 3-2. Motivation Toolkit Goal #1: During Stage

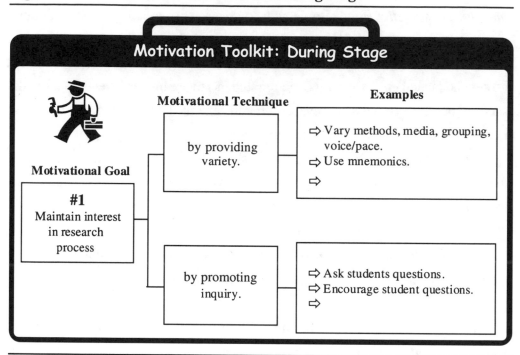

We return to the Motivation Overlay and move on to the next motivational goal in the During Stage of research: **to promote the value of learning information skills.**

Figure 3-3. Motivational Goal #2: During Stage

Research Stages	During
Information Skills	Exploration Collection Organization
Motivational Goals	Maintain interest in the research process ✓ **Promote value of information skills** Reinforce confidence in research ability
Related Motivational Theories	Expectancy-value Need Flow Attribution Social learning

We've identified the following techniques for accomplishing this goal:

- ◆ maintaining relevance of learning information skills
- ◆ modeling effective research skills
- ◆ allowing choices for learning information skills

A number of motivational strategies are included in the following description of these techniques.

Promoting the Value of Information Skills

Maintaining relevance of acquiring information skills to attain current and future goals helps to sustain their *value* to students. Students like learning something that offers them a benefit or a real advantage (Wlodkowski, 1981). There are many ways this can be accomplished. For example, throughout the school year students could keep a diary of all the ways using information skills has benefited them; this is especially good for students who are high in need for achievement and derive satisfaction from monitoring their personal growth. Students could form small groups to share ideas on how information skills could be used in their everyday lives, a strategy particularly well suited to those who are high in need for affiliation. Students could lead a brainstorming session of ways information skills might be used in other school activities and assignments; students high in need for power enjoy opportunities to provide leadership.

Another way to provide relevance is to help students connect familiar concepts to new, more abstract concepts to be learned. *Analogies* are particularly powerful for doing this. For example, you could teach students the concept  of "synthesis" by comparing it to assembling a model airplane or baking a cake. In both activities, you must take various parts or ingredients and put them together in such a way that they form a new and coherent whole. You could also provide *examples* of new concepts or procedures, such as teaching the information problem-solving process using a common activity such as choosing which movie to go to on Saturday night, determining what courses to take next year, or deciding whom to ask to the prom. One LMS we know used a humorous example to teach the concept of "evaluation." She related this story to a fourth grade class: "The first brownies I made from scratch were gorgeous. I had four brothers and they couldn't wait to stuff those brownies in their mouths. Well, they almost gagged. I thought the recipe said to use one cup of salt, but it said *one teaspoon*. The recipe was in my mother's handwriting and she had curved the 't' just a little too much. That's when they learned I needed glasses. We evaluated my work and it didn't pass." The students giggled as she related her story and introduced them to the importance of evaluation in an enjoyable and memorable way.

One of the most effective ways to promote the value of information skills is *to link them to current classroom activities and assignments*. Barbara Toumbacaris used this method with a group of tenth graders in the next Motivational Moment.

▶ Motivational Moment

Library Media Specialist:	**Barbara Toumbacaris**
School:	G. Ray Bodley High School, Fulton, New York
Grade Level:	10
Instructional Goal:	To find biographical sources on and song lyrics by musicians
Information Skills:	Exploration, Collection
Motivational Goal:	To promote value of information skills

One of the English teachers in my school has come to the library for many years to ask the LMS to pull all the books on musicians and put them on a cart so that when he brings his students to the library media center, they can use them to do their research. Their assignment was to research on a certain musician and to locate and review the lyrics of a song by that musician. The teacher seemed open to new ways of handling this assignment. The kids typically think they know how to do this and do not need help, but sometimes that's not the case. So I planned a lesson to teach them how to locate and access print and electronic information for their assignment.

I used an easel board and wrote on one large poster paper the research steps and on another a list of sources grouped by "electronic" and "print." We discussed what print resources were available in the library media center (mostly biographies and reference books) but when I mentioned finding articles, they didn't seem to know what to do. Using a computer and projector, I asked students for names of some of the musicians they were researching. I then typed the names into an Internet search program and the students seemed really interested in the information we retrieved. I also had found some websites where you could type in the musician's name and get lyrics. One student exclaimed, "I didn't know it could be this easy!" They thought it would be an overwhelming thing to find. They were definitely impressed!

Barbara's lesson certainly reinforced the value of information skills, particularly in terms of their class assignment. The students learned how various information resources work and how those sources can help them solve their information problems, saving them time, effort, and a lot of frustration. The strategies Barbara used also were a lot more interesting than just searching a stack of books on a cart, and her website demonstration helped fortify their research confidence.

In another example of a creative information skills lesson that maintained the relevance of information skills, the LMS tied her instruction to a classroom unit on the Middle Ages for a combined third and fourth grade class. She began by showing the students a string of glass beads made in Venice, Italy, that she had received as a gift. She described how one became a glassblower in the Middle Ages by first becoming an "apprentice." After you had worked with a master glassblower for seven years, you became a "journeyman." Once you had become skilled enough to create a recognized "masterpiece," you could then set up your own shop. She then told the students they were about to become "apprentice librarians," adding with a smile that it would take far less than the usual seven years to be trained. She further explained that master craftsmen were often very secretive about their skills, but librarians will share their skills and be helpful to everyone so they can find what they need. This lesson maintained a sense of relevance for students by extending the instruction they were receiving in the classroom in a way that brought some of the concepts to life so that these young students could easily understand.

Modeling effective research skills is another technique for promoting the value of information skills. Good and Brophy (1994) maintain that students often learn more effectively by observing through modeling than by direct instruction. It is especially important in the During Stage of the research process, once students have identified a range of information sources related to their topic; have begun to read, view, or listen to the information contained within each source; and have started gathering relevant information for their research projects. This requires students to extract information that may entail such skills as note taking, speaking into a tape recorder, and cutting and pasting electronic information.

The problem occurs when students try extracting information and putting it into their own words. Teaching them accuracy without copying is challenging and students may lack confidence in their ability to do this. Where does modeling come in? Practicing this skill with students and providing them with a range of models from you or other students will help students learn this important skill. One approach to doing this is to model the critical thinking processes involved in information extraction by "talking aloud" as you actually go through the process. This approach helps your students (1) gain insight about what you are thinking and feeling, and (2) learn how to apply what they see to their own experiences.

Do you remember in Chapter One when we discussed modeling as a manifestation of social learning theory? We described how you can provide a role model for your students through your enthusiasm toward learning to use information skills. But there are others who can also serve as models to accomplish this Motivational Goal. For example, high school students can speak to middle school students about how they use information skills to complete their assignments. Parents and other adults in the community can provide testimonials on how they use information skills to do their jobs better. Students within the class who have mastered certain skills can model these skills to other students in the class.

A final technique that helps to promote the value of information skills is to *allow students to make choices* when working on a research project. Choice is a way for students to inject variety into their task and to have some control over it. Deci (1995) suggests that giving students choices about the way they will learn or perform will enhance their feelings of self-determination and autonomy and increase intrinsic motivation. If you need to control the range of choices you give your students, you could provide a list of alternatives from which they can choose or, otherwise, just let them decide any or all of the following parameters of the task:

- ◆ their topic
- ◆ the length of time to complete the assignment
- ◆ the method for communicating the results
- ◆ the number or type of sources they will use
- ◆ whether they will complete the project individually, with a partner, or in small groups
- ◆ the criteria on which their research results will be assessed

Giving students as much control as possible over their own research task increases both the personal value of that task and their confidence in their ability to successfully complete it. Our next Motivational Moment illustrates how Barb Grady found a creative way to offer her students options for solving a problem that entailed taking an old technology and using it in new ways.

▶ **Motivational Moment**

Library Media Specialist:	**Barbara Grady**
School Name & Location:	Enosburg Elementary School, Enosburg Falls, Vermont
Grade Level:	6
Instructional Goal:	To explore a range of categorization schemes for information resources
Information Skill:	Organization
Motivational Goal:	To promote the value of information skills

I have been trying to give away drawers of filmstrips that no one uses anymore. I put them out at a teachers' meeting and they didn't go because they weren't organized and no one had time to look through. So I gave the problem to the sixth grade as an organizing activity. I gave each group a tray of filmstrips and asked the group to organize them any way they wanted to, but they needed to explain their reasoning to the whole group. We then talked about the different ways this "information" was synthesized in the small groups—categories, alphabetically, color, date, etc., and that information (e.g., filmstrips) can be arranged in various ways. The students found that organizing and eventually "packaging" these information resources actually made them desirable to teachers. It is amazing how this simple activity took off and got the kids excited about information problem solving!

When Barb let her students work in groups, she was satisfying their need for affiliation. Most likely they brainstormed a variety of options for organizing the filmstrips. The fact that the task would eventually result in something useful for the teachers in the school provided a motivating reward tied to the task that is likely to lead to satisfaction and continuing motivation. We can now add the next piece to our Motivation Toolkit.

Figure 3-4. Motivation Toolkit Goal #2: During Stage

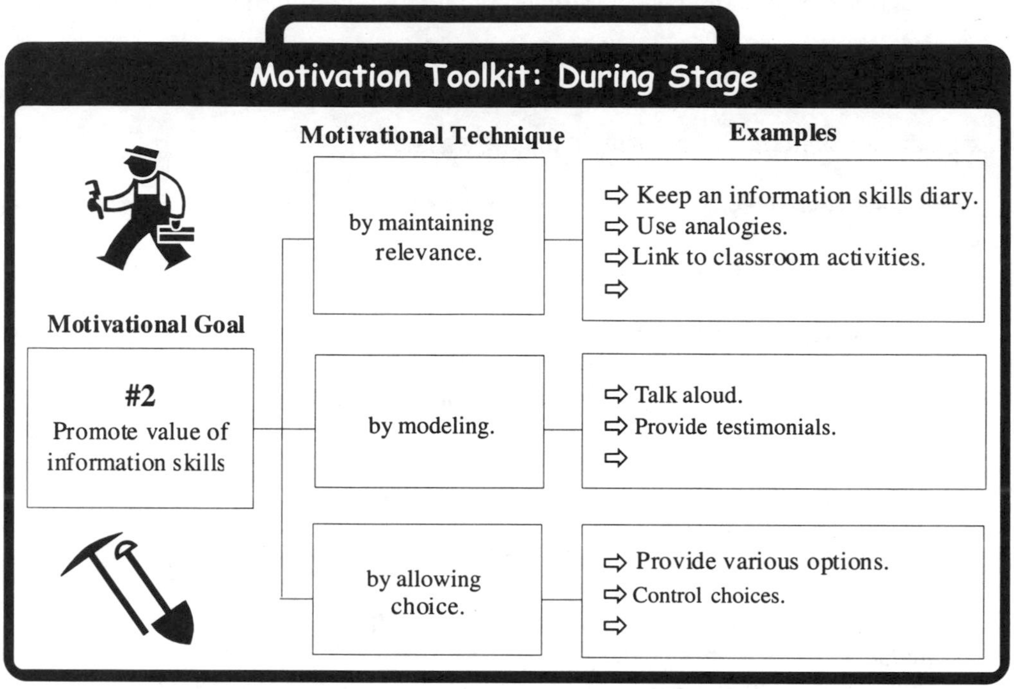

Motivation Toolkit: During Stage

Motivational Technique

Examples

Motivational Goal

#2
Promote value of information skills

by maintaining relevance.

⇨ Keep an information skills diary.
⇨ Use analogies.
⇨ Link to classroom activities.
⇨

by modeling.

⇨ Talk aloud.
⇨ Provide testimonials.
⇨

by allowing choice.

⇨ Provide various options.
⇨ Control choices.
⇨

We have now reached the Motivation Overlay's final Motivational Goal for the During Stage of the research process: **to reinforce students' expectations for success by strengthening their confidence in their research abilities**.

Figure 3-5. Motivational Goal #3: During Stage

Research Stages	During
Information Skills	Exploration Collection Organization
Motivational Goals	Maintain interest in the research process Promote value of information skills ✓ **Reinforce confidence in research ability**
Related Motivational Theories	Expectancy-value Need Flow Attribution Social learning

We recommend the following techniques for accomplishing this goal:

◆ providing opportunities for success

◆ maintaining an atmosphere of acceptance

◆ recognizing success and improvement

A number of motivational strategies related to each technique are included in the discussion.

Reinforcing Confidence in Research Ability

In the During Stage it is crucial to maintain and reinforce the confidence built in the Beginning Stage of the research process. The early portion of the During Stage of research is one in which students form a research focus and begin to locate and explore specific information sources. In this part of the process, students will likely be learning to use a number of searching tools, both print and electronic, and although these tools share some common searching features, many have their own unique characteristics. This causes a "double whammy" of ambiguity for students—doubt about which tools to use and how to use them and uncertainty about their ability to identify and find the information they need. Kuhlthau (1993) characterizes this part of the research process as one of the most difficult for students, when feelings of confusion, anxiety, and uncertainty tend to increase and their expectations for success begin to decrease. This is a critical point in the motivation of students, particularly for those who have a low expectation for success.

Brophy (1998) cites apathy, resignation, and resentment as resulting attitudes for low-expectancy students. Low-achieving students often develop anxiety as a result of repeated failures and low expectations for success (Wigfield and Eccles, 1998). This would seem to demand greater use of confidence-building strategies at this point in the research process. Yet, in a research study to determine the amount and types (using Keller's ARCS Model) of motivational strategies used by LMSs during their information skills instruction, only 15% of all motivation strategies used by the library media specialists were intended to build and reinforce students' confidence (Small, 1999). Furthermore, elementary LMSs used fewer confidence strategies than middle school LMSs at a time when these young and inexperienced students were just beginning to test their research skills and abilities and might need them the most.

One effective way of maintaining high student confidence is to **provide opportunities for success**. Three potential ways of accomplishing this are:

◆ having students practice newly learned skills on simpler information problems that prepare them for a larger, more difficult research project

◆ breaking a complex learning task up into smaller, more manageable chunks

◆ in early research projects, providing explicit guidelines and help mechanisms to ensure learning success

One LMS we know uses a scavenger hunt to help her fourth grade beginning researchers to locate the information resources they will need for their first research projects. The students work in pairs to seek the items on the scavenger hunt list. As they proceed, they begin to discover a number of location and access concepts, such as how books are shelved, the fact that call numbers do not always contain actual numbers, etc. Another LMS turns her fifth grade students into "research detectives" for their first research project on the Iroquois Confederacy. She provides an outline of the important questions related to their research topic that, as detectives, they must investigate (for example, what clothing did they wear? What foods did they eat? What festivals did they celebrate?). Around the room she places pictures to provide clues to where specific information might be found. Both of these examples illustrate ways to allow students to practice their information skills through a low-anxiety, enjoyable learning activity.

Another confidence-reinforcing strategy is to work with classroom teachers to structure learning tasks and assignments at progressively difficult levels of research challenges. As students practice their information problem-solving skills, first in simple exercises and assignments and then in more difficult activities and projects, they begin to internalize the process, becoming increasingly competent and ultimately more confident about their ability to be successful researchers.

In the following Motivational Moment, Paula Brown provides an interesting type of activity that fortified her students' confidence as they prepared for an upcoming field trip.

▶ Motivational Moment

Library Media Specialist: **Paula Brown**
School Name & Location: The Episcopal Academy,
Merion, Pennsylvania
Grade Level: 5
Instructional Goal: To gather information about the cultural and religious aspects of the Middle East
Information Skills: Exploration, Collection
Motivational Goal: To reinforce confidence in students' research abilities

The fifth grade teachers in my school wanted their students to be exposed to some of the cultural and religious aspects of the Middle East so they planned a visit to a local mosque. Before the visit, teachers wanted students to be prepared with some knowledge about what they would see and hear. So, students were placed in groups of three and given a specific list of four different images to identify for fellow students. Examples included specific mosques, specific markets, oil rigs, or pipelines (which I identified through a presearch of encyclopedias), a minaret, the Kaaba, veiled women, etc.

Students were asked how they would find each image and an opportunity was given to look up each specific term with limited luck. To prevent them from becoming discouraged, I asked them to brainstorm for other connected words, which they did and came up with more general terms like mosque, Arab, Muslim, Middle East, under which they could find the specific picture by exploring whatever pictures are available under the broad term like "mosque."

Because online image searching is risky for this grade level, I preselected sites for image searching and posted to my elementary homepage or used a safe search site as a reward after a student found the hard copy. This ensured that students would find the information they needed. Students used indexes, found pictures, and read captions to determine if they were the images that they sought, copied or marked the spot, and presented the information to the other students. Students left the library with bolstered feelings of confidence in their ability to locate the information they needed. When they visited the mosque, teachers (and their host) were very pleased not only by the students' knowledge but also their enthusiasm about the subject.

Paula did several things to ensure that her students had a successful learning experience. She worked with teachers to plan the activity to make sure it was consistent with their instructional goals. She interceded with a keyword brainstorming activity at a critical moment when students might have become discouraged in their information search. Finally, she alerted students to relevant websites so they would be able to quickly and easily find the information they needed. Since this lesson was *not* intended to make sure students could *find* the information they needed but was intended to make sure students could *use* that information, this was an appropriate form of help.

Although our overall goal is to develop *independent* users of information and ideas, there are times when we must be available to help and guide students during the research process. Providing help to students when needed does not mean *doing the work* for them. But, particularly with students who are just getting their "research feet" wet or those with learning difficulties, a supportive learning environment that ***maintains an atmosphere of acceptance,*** in which students are not afraid to try new ways to explore their environment and express their discoveries, experience success (and failure), and develop research competence early on, is an important motivational factor in reinforcing students' confidence in their research abilities. This often means being available for help at times other than when their class visits the library media center. Here's another Motivational Moment from Jan Chemotti, who did just that.

▶ Motivational Moment

Library Media Specialist:	**Jan Chemotti**
School Name & Location:	West Genesee Middle School, Camillus, New York
Grade Level:	8
Instructional Goal:	To extract information from print and electronic sources
Information Skills:	Collection, Organization
Motivational Goal:	To reinforce confidence in students' research abilities

Our eighth grade interdisciplinary project (we call it "The Travel Project") involves every core subject in the eighth grade curriculum. One of my roles in the project is to teach the students to use the software called "Tripmaker" produced by Rand McNally. It is a complex type of software so I spend a few days teaching students how the software works. The project stretches over a four-month period and students have many steps to complete during that time.

They must use the mapping software to produce a final product that contains (1) a detailed map with directions for driving on an imaginary trip each student will take within the 50 states—some students drive to Florida, others to California; some board a plane to Hawaiii and tour an island by car. They decide what routes they will end up taking and calculate the amount of time on each route and the duration of the whole trip; (2) a map that has historic sites labeled on the driving route; and (3) a map with tourist sites labeled that are on the driving route.

Once students have a clear idea as to the parameters of the assignment, they come to the library to learn how to operate the software. They know that this software is the key resource they will need because, besides spreadsheets, charts, and graphs for other parts of the project, they need to use the software to produce their maps. Once they have learned how the software works and what the overall concept is, then they're required to use the library and our resources— tour guides, geographic resources, atlases, books about the states—to find historic sites and tourist attractions.

At about midway through the process, it's time to sit down and do their labeling and some students realize they have forgotten how to operate the software. Because the software is so detailed and involved, they can get lost, not know where they're going, or lose all the maps they have produced. This causes them to get very frustrated and lose interest, often just giving up. So I offered them the opportunity to come into the library after school one day a week where I would reteach the software to them in smaller groups. We called it "refresher time." I went through step by step, showing them where to go and how to do each function. Then each student would state his or her specific problem, we would determine if it was a common problem, and we would try to solve it. I went around to each computer and said, "You're exactly where you should be" or "You need to do this." These kids tend to give up easily and say they can't do something. After about an hour with me, they had a lot of confidence when they were finished.

They were able to come in and work independently afterward. A little refresher went a long way!

Often, when learning abstract or concept concepts or procedures, students need additional instruction to fortify their skills as well as their confidence so that they can be successful. ("Additional" does not mean more content but usually involves repetition of previous instruction, presented in different ways and reinforced with supplementary materials such as help sheets.) Some LMSs, like Jan, provide an atmosphere of acceptance and support through special "help periods" when any student can come in for individual guidance. These may be before and/or after school, during lunch periods, or any designated time during the school day when the LMS is available to devote full time to this endeavor. By calling it "refresher time," Jan is sensitive to adolescent fears that their peers might think they are "stupid" or "goofing off."

Some students, particularly adolescents, may be reluctant to ask for help when their peers are present but will often do so in a private, one-on-one situation. Finding times for individual students to come to the library media center for help (or just assurance that they are doing things right) is critical for these students. Harold Geneen, chief executive officer of IT&T, once said, "The best way to inspire people to superior performance is to convince them by everything you do and by your everyday attitude that you are wholeheartedly supporting them" (1984).

Another idea we had for reinforcing students' confidence in their research abilities builds on a type of assignment we often hear about from practitioners, particularly those at the high school level. It is the year-end assignment in which students are required to write a major research paper (most often for a history or English class), using a variety of information sources (including electronic). Students soon become overwhelmed and anxious because they don't know how to identify the best information sources available in the myriad forms available to them. So our idea is early in the fall to start teaching them ways to evaluate a wide range of resources, using or adapting existing evaluation tools for assessing both print resources and electronic resources. Even young children can learn to do this well.

Although there are many assessment tools for evaluating resources, few are designed specifically for use by children. Recently, the authors developed a series of evaluation instruments to determine the motivational quality of World Wide Web sites, known as WebMAC© (Website Motivational Analysis Checklist) evaluation instruments, several of which are designed for use by students. They are intended to empower students with control over the selection and use of information resources for solving their information problems.

WebMAC Junior is aimed at students in grades one through four; *WebMAC Middle* targets fifth through eighth graders; *WebMAC Senior* is intended for high school and college students. These instruments go beyond the typical content-focused evaluation instruments and include such motivation-related elements as functionality and appeal. They identify four critical descriptors of website quality: stimulating, meaningful, organized, and easy to use. What makes these instruments unique is that they:

♦ are grounded in motivation theory

♦ are designed for use by students

♦ help users interpret the results so they can be used for improvement

(For more information on the WebMAC© instruments and ideas for using them, consult Small and Arnone's *WWW Motivation Mining: Finding Treasures for Teaching Evaluation Skills* (*Grade 1–6*) and *WWW Motivation Mining: Finding Treasures for Teaching Evaluation Skills* (*Grades 7–12*), published by Linworth.

We have used these evaluation instruments with students at all levels with great success. For example, early in the school year you could have students practice using these types of evaluation tools with various resources until the process becomes familiar and comfortable. Then, by the time an actual research project is assigned, students will feel quite expert at assessing the quality of the resources they encounter.

Evaluating information resources (and the information they find within them) is an important critical thinking skill for students at all grade levels. Needless to say, competence in resource evaluation goes a long way toward increasing confidence and ensuring an expectation for successful achievement of the research assignment.

A final strategy for reinforcing students' confidence in their research abilities is to **recognize success and improvement** throughout the learning process. One way to do this is through *motivational feedback* that encourages students, expresses pride in their accomplishments, and ties those accomplishments to effort and skill. Frymier (1974) describes two styles of feedback. One is a positive style in which teachers feed a steady stream of positive, encouraging statements to students as they are learning. Brophy (1998) suggests that feedback should encourage persistence and patience rather than praise hard work (e.g., "Keep at it—you're doing fine" or "Yes, this is hard, but look how much you have done already"). The other is negative in nature (e.g., "For goodness sake, haven't you finished yet?" "You'd better pay attention or you won't learn"). It is easy to guess which type of feedback reinforces learning confidence and which undermines it.

Recognizing individual student *achievement*, even if it is learning something very basic or small, can go a long way toward reinforcing that student's self-esteem. Recognition can come in the form of praise, either one-on-one or in the group, or more tangible rewards such as gold stars or "happy-grams" (notes on a student's accomplishment that go home to parents). Brophy warns that some students find it embarrassing to be praised in front of their peers and prefer it to be done in private.

Remember the LMS we described earlier in this chapter who taught a lesson on the Middle Ages by forming a "Library Guild"? She also found a way to reward learning progress. She gave each student a printed handout entitled "Steps to Becoming a Master of the Library Guild." She then told the class that every time they accomplished one of the 48 learning tasks on the form related to their classroom assignments on the Middle Ages, they could record it on their handout. Some examples of these tasks are:

- understanding the difference between keyword, author, title, and subject searches

- finding information in atlases

- using the online catalog to locate books at other libraries

- explaining how a table of contents works

- presenting a booktalk for class

Each time students came to the library media center, they could work on the various skills, and as they reached different levels of proficiency, they were rewarded with a promotion from apprentice to journeyman and, eventually, to the highest level, master. As students progressed to higher levels of competence and skill, their learning confidence was bolstered. The LMS provided an enjoyable way to reinforce students' confidence in their library and information skills that not only linked directly to their classroom assignments but also built on some of the specific concepts they were learning in the classroom.

In addition to recognizing an individual's achievement of a research task, we also advocate recognizing individual *improvement*, especially progress and persistence. This is particularly important for students who may need more time and help in learning information skills. These students need encouragement and support for even small successes. Such reinforcement can come from a variety of sources. It can come from the instructor; it can come from other students, a strategy that helps strengthen peer relationships (particularly those high in need for affiliation); and it can come from within the student him- or herself, indicating an awareness of his or her progress and achievement.

It is also important to provide *informative feedback* that students can use to improve and eventually achieve. Such feedback must focus on the research task (e.g., "Your references need to have a consistent format. You might want to use this style manual as a guide for creating your bibliography") rather than the student's ability (e.g., "You must not have checked the style manual before you developed your bibliography. You need to relearn how to construct a bibliography correctly"). By doing so, the student will understand the importance of effort and not lose confidence in his or her research capabilities. Attributing any improvement or success to hard work and to gaining needed skills will help prevent or overcome the learned helplessness and low expectations for success some students may have as a result of past failures.

The last part of your Motivation Toolkit for the During Stage of research appears on the next page. It includes each of the goals presented in the Motivation Overlay and the techniques and example strategies we have described in the preceding sections.

Figure 3-6. Motivation Toolkit Goal #3: During Stage

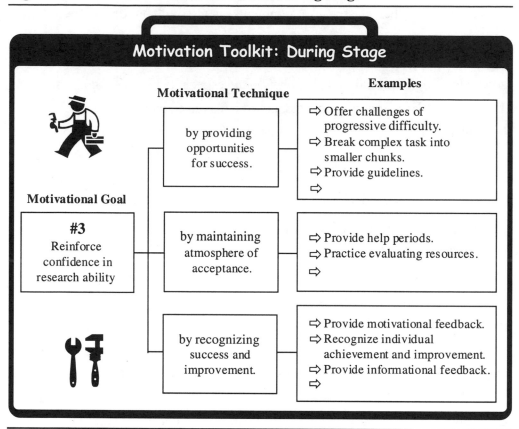

Again, you are encouraged to add your own ideas for strategies that have worked for you or that you think might be effective in the future. The entire Motivation Toolkit for the During Stage is presented on the following page.

Figure 3-7. Motivation Toolkit: During Stage

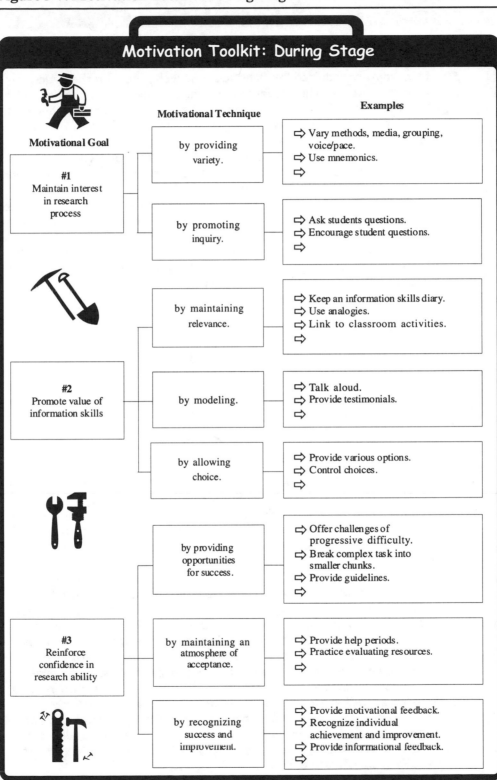

Motivation Toolkit: During Stage

Motivational Goal	Motivational Technique	Examples
#1 Maintain interest in research process	by providing variety.	⇨ Vary methods, media, grouping, voice/pace. ⇨ Use mnemonics. ⇨
	by promoting inquiry.	⇨ Ask students questions. ⇨ Encourage student questions. ⇨
#2 Promote value of information skills	by maintaining relevance.	⇨ Keep an information skills diary. ⇨ Use analogies. ⇨ Link to classroom activities. ⇨
	by modeling.	⇨ Talk aloud. ⇨ Provide testimonials. ⇨
	by allowing choice.	⇨ Provide various options. ⇨ Control choices. ⇨
#3 Reinforce confidence in research ability	by providing opportunities for success.	⇨ Offer challenges of progressive difficulty. ⇨ Break complex task into smaller chunks. ⇨ Provide guidelines. ⇨
	by maintaining an atmosphere of acceptance.	⇨ Provide help periods. ⇨ Practice evaluating resources. ⇨
	by recognizing success and improvement.	⇨ Provide motivational feedback. ⇨ Recognize individual achievement and improvement. ⇨ Provide informational feedback. ⇨

What Would YOU Do?

? During the spring semester, all of the eleventh grade students in the school are required to complete a research paper for their American history class. The students can come to the library media center during their free periods to work. The LMS notices that, while most of the students are working on their papers, Juan, a gifted and generally hardworking student, seems to be doing anything but ... talking to friends, reading a Stephen King novel, doing other homework. When the LMS approaches Juan and asks him why he isn't working on his research paper, he states, "Look, I just can't write this paper. Anyway, why should I? Last year, the paper I wrote was bad. I wasn't particularly interested in the topic so I spent almost no time on it—I blew it off—and I got an 'A'! Last semester I chose a topic I really liked and worked hard on it—I would even go so far as to say I had fun writing it. But when the teacher handed it back, there was a big 'D' on it. Why should I even bother this semester? It obviously doesn't matter whether I work hard on it or not; it's out of my control!" **What would you do?**

! *Although it is possible that the eleventh grade history teachers in the school do not grade fairly, it is much more likely that Juan has developed a learned helplessness attitude toward research. His past experiences reinforce his belief that no matter what he does, he cannot control the outcomes of his behavior. If possible, you could take Juan's two past papers and go over them with him, providing informative feedback about what he did wrong (and right) and attributing it to either his hard work or skills. The "A" paper might have been better than he perceived it or the assignment may have been too easy, lacked challenge, and required a minimum of effort on Juan's part—which is what he gave it. The "D" paper may have merely been the result of not following the specifications of the assignment, rather than an inability to write a research paper. However, if Juan does lack some of the skills necessary to successfully complete the assignment, you need to find ways to help him work on those skills, such as one-on-one tutoring (with you or with a student who has mastered the process), providing small research tasks that allow him to practice needed skills, showing him exemplary papers and helping him compare his work to identify specific areas in need of more effort.*

Motivational Makeover

It's time to show you another Motivational Makeover, this time by Marilyn Day, an English teacher from Montrose, Pennsylvania. Building learning confidence may be especially challenging when working with low-achieving students. Marilyn used some interesting motivational techniques she learned in one of our motivation seminars to turn a key instructional plan into a meaningful experience for a special group of students. Her Lackluster Lesson Plan appears on the next page.

▶Lackluster Lesson Plan

Audience: Eleventh graders

Topic: Careers

Instructional Goal: To use various information resources to learn about careers

Information Skills: Definition, Selection, Planning, Exploration, Collection, Organization

Procedures:

1. Give students a handout describing their career reports and what they are required to do in terms of length, format, outlines, and due dates.

2. Talk about the handout, telling them what they will be doing in the library.

3. When the class arrives in the library, give them a booklet with examples of note cards and bibliography cards.

4. Point out to students where they might find materials on their career.

5. Students spend several days searching and taking notes from the sources.

6. Students will compile a stack of bibliography cards.

7. After taking notes, student will do a formal typed outline.

8. Students will then work during class in writing workshops to write two drafts of their report.

9. Students will then be left on their own to type up the final report.

Before revising her lesson, Marilyn thought carefully about her learning audience, the goals of her lesson, and her school's upcoming Job Fair. Here are her thoughts.

"This is a class that is made up largely of learning-disabled students, vocational students, and low achievers. By eleventh grade many of these students are very burned out and they know that they are 'tracked' into the lower-skills English class. It even says 'Life Skills English' on their schedules. This class is also scheduled during the last period of the day, so keeping the students on task is very hard to do most of the time. Many of these students have been to vocational school in the morning and they have had a very long day.

"Another area of concern for these students is their total lack of confidence in what they can do. By eleventh grade they have had so many failure situations that many of them will not try anything. Some students will literally do nothing; so getting them to work on this project would be a wonderful thing for them in terms of success and in terms of thinking about their future.

"This lesson takes about two to three weeks from start to finish, with several days researching in the library and writing workshop time given back in the classroom. Even though many of these students are interested in finding out about a career of their choice, the lesson is too hard for them to stay on task and to stay motivated. This unit needs to be shorter and broken down into smaller tasks so that these students feel that they can succeed at finding information in the library. Also, this lesson involves too many areas that they have to access in the library; there should be a more limited focus of what areas they need to research."

Keeping all of this in mind, Marilyn developed her Motivational Makeover, which begins on the next page. Although Marilyn estimates the entire lesson will take two to three weeks, she has focused on the five days devoted to the research task. We think you'll agree that her new plan will go a long way toward solving her motivational "challenge."

► **Marilyn's Motivational Makeover**

Audience: Eleventh graders

Topic: Careers

Instructional Goal: To use various information resources to learn about careers

Information Skills: Definition, Selection, Planning, Exploration, Collection, Organization, Presentation

Motivational Goals: To promote value of information skills. To build and reinforce confidence in their research abilities.

Motivational Measures: Observed excitement about task. Interest in content. Time on task. Satisfaction with the finished product.

Lesson Plan:

Day One: In class, using poster board and old magazines or anything applicable, have the students make up a "This Is Your Life" collage of pictures that they feel will depict their life in 10 years' time. Or, what they would like their life to look like or be like in 10 years' time. They can include things to show their future: house, car, wife or husband or "significant other," their kids, their vacation destinations, anything that shows what they want and where they want to be 10 years down the road. However, they must write in bold across the top of their poster board, the job or career that they will be doing that will provide the means to get all of the "goodies" in the collage pictures. Then, at the end of the period, have them share their collages and talk to the class about the picture of what their life will be like. But do not tell them what the "This Is Your Life" collage is for or in any way suggest that they are going to do a "horrible, awful, research project." Then, simply hang the collages around the room.

Days Two-Three: The next day in class, tell the students that they are going on a job hunt to look for ideas, facts, and information that will help them make their "This Is Your Life" collage become a reality. Then take them to the library media center where you and the LMS have assembled on a shelf all of the encyclopedias, books, and magazines on careers. Then allow them to explore, collect, and organize data on their careers.

Day Four: Give each student a three-sided presentation board and tell them to get ready for the Job Fair. On one of the three sides of the presentation board they can use their original collage. They can write up

continued on next page

▶ Marilyn's Motivational Makeover (continued)

and present the information that they have on the outline on another one of the three sides, and the last side of the board they can use to present their job in any fashion or manner that they wish, again through pictures, stories, etc. Then tell the students that they will be discussing and setting up a desk tomorrow with their presentation boards and that they will be the "Job Expert" about their career at the Job Fair. These students have a very low opinion of how well they think they can do in a library; so, the main strategy here is to give them a predeveloped outline where they can readily fill in the information.

Day Five: This is Job Fair Day. Prearrange with a junior high teacher to have her seventh or eighth grade classes come to your Job Fair. The junior high students can go around to the different desks and presentation boards and ask questions of the eleventh graders about their job or career. The junior high teacher could even have prepared questions that her students have to ask the career students. Hopefully, this would be very rewarding to this eleventh grade class since they are the type of students that never get a chance to be an expert on anything.

Since raising the confidence level of her students was so important, Marilyn used several motivational strategies to help build her students' competence and self-esteem. She:

- ◆ adjusted the level of challenge of the learning task so that it was challenging but attainable
- ◆ allowed students to choose a topic that had personal meaning to them and real-life application
- ◆ provided learning support by organizing appropriate resources and creating a sample outline (an example of vicarious observation modeling as described in Chapter One)
- ◆ made students be responsible for their own learning by acting as "experts" to showcase their knowledge to others in a nonthreatening way

As students progressed, they became more confident in their knowledge and skills.

Providing a supportive learning environment, like Marilyn's, that includes reassurance and encouragement is especially important when working with lower-ability students or students with learning disabilities on a homework assignment or project. These students have often experienced failure in their educational lives, and the main challenge is to try to build (or rebuild) their confidence in their ability to complete the assignment successfully. Frequently these students have a high external locus of control and see little connection between their effort and successful outcomes. A learning environment, like the one Marilyn provided, where students can safely explore and develop their information skills and have fun while they are doing it will likely result in increased effort and confidence, ultimately bringing them more pleasure in their learning and motivating them to produce quality work.

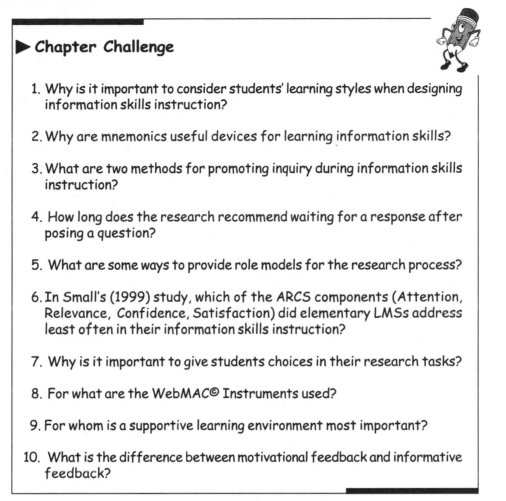

▶ **Chapter Challenge**

1. Why is it important to consider students' learning styles when designing information skills instruction?

2. Why are mnemonics useful devices for learning information skills?

3. What are two methods for promoting inquiry during information skills instruction?

4. How long does the research recommend waiting for a response after posing a question?

5. What are some ways to provide role models for the research process?

6. In Small's (1999) study, which of the ARCS components (Attention, Relevance, Confidence, Satisfaction) did elementary LMSs address least often in their information skills instruction?

7. Why is it important to give students choices in their research tasks?

8. For what are the WebMAC© Instruments used?

9. For whom is a supportive learning environment most important?

10. What is the difference between motivational feedback and informative feedback?

▶ Chapter Challenge: Answers

1. A variety of learning styles requires varying the methods, media, and materials used in instruction. Variety is one technique for maintaining students' interest in learning information skills.

2. Mnemonics help students remember important content in a way that is fun and useful.

3. You can pose questions to students or encourage students to ask questions of you and/or the class.

4. Three to five seconds.

5. We've suggested inviting high school students to share their information problem-solving experiences with middle school students, having parents or other adults provide testimonials on how they use information skills in their jobs, and asking students who have mastered one or more skills to demonstrate using those skills to other students. Can you think of other ways to provide "research role models"?

6. Confidence.

7. It provides variety in and a shared control over their own learning, which can enhance their feelings of self-determination and autonomy and increase their intrinsic motivation.

8. The WebMAC© instruments are designed for use by students to evaluate the websites they encounter as information sources. Evaluating information and information resources is an important critical thinking skill for students at all grade levels.

9. A supportive learning environment is particularly important for students who are just learning the research process or those with learning difficulties.

10. Motivational feedback provides encouragement, expresses pride in their accomplishments, and ties those accomplishments to effort and skill. Informative feedback provides information that students can use to improve their research skills and eventually achieve the research task.

Reflection Points

Please use this page to record your ideas and special points to remember from Chapter Three.

References

Brophy, J., *Motivating Students to Learn* (Boston: McGraw Hill, 1998).

Davidson, G.V., "Matching Learning Styles with Teaching Styles: Is It a Useful Concept in Instruction?" *Performance & Instruction* (Apr. 1990): 36-38.

Deci. E.L., *Why We Do What We Do: Understanding Self-Motivation* (New York: Penguin Books, 1995).

Frymier, Jack R., *Motivation and Learning in School* 43 (Bloomington, IN: Phi Delta Kappa Educational Foundation, 1974).

Geneen, Harold, *Managing* (New York: Doubleday, 1984).

Good, T.L., and J.E. Brophy, *Looking in Classrooms*, 6th ed. (New York: HarperCollins, 1994).

Joyce, Marilyn Z., and Julie I. Tallman, *Making the Writing and Research Connection with the I-Search Process: A How-to Do-It Manual for Teachers and School Librarians* (New York: Neal-Schuman, 1997).

Kuhlthau, Carol, *Teaching the Library Research Process* (West Nyack, NY: The Center for Applied Research in Education, 1985).

———, "Inside the Search Process: Information Seeking from the User's Perspective," *Journal of the American Society of Information Science* 42, no. 5 (1991): 361-371.

———, "Implementing a Process Approach to Information Skills: A Study Identifying Indicators of Success in Library Media Programs," *School Library Media Quarterly* 22, no. 1 (1993): 11-18.

Locke, J., From "Some Thoughts Concerning Education" (1692): Part IX, Section 148. In *Internet Modern History Sourcebook* <http:www.fordham.edu/halsall/mod/1692locke-education.html>

Macrorie, Ken, *The I-Search Process* (Portsmouth, NH: Heinemann, 1988).

Rowe, Mary Budd, "Wait Time: Slowing Down May Be a Way of Speeding Up!" *Journal of Teacher Education* 37, no. 1 (1986): 43-50.

Small, Ruth V., "An Exploration of Motivational Strategies Used by Library Media Specialists During Library and Information Skills Instruction," *School Library Media Research* 2 (1999).

Warner, Richard L., "How Do Bears Measure Up?" *School Library Media Activities Monthly* XIV, no. 6 (1998).

Wigfield, A., and J. Eccles, "Test Anxiety in Elementary and Secondary School Students," *Educational Psychologist* 24 (1998): 159-83.

Wlodkowski, Raymond J., "Making Sense out of Motivation: A Systematic Model to Consolidate Motivational Constructs Across Theories," *Educational Psychologist* 16, no. 2 (1981): 101-10.

Zorfass, Judith M., *Make It Happen! Inquiry and Technology in the Middle School Curriculum* (Newton, MA: Education Development Center, 1991).

Chapter Four

... An Ending

> **"** By instructing in a manner that supports intrinsic motivation,
> we not only stand a chance to develop lifelong learners but
> also to contribute to the positive evolution of our own
> discipline. **"**

~ Raymond J. Wlodkowski, 1993, p. 288

Introduction

An ending can lead to a new **beginning.** If we as educators and information professionals are successful in promoting students' excitement about research, then the resolution of one research question should motivate students to begin exploring yet another question. Perhaps it is a question that extends the completed research project or a point of interest that cropped up in the course of the research. It may even be an unrelated question, but the successful research experience has students believing in their own abilities as young researchers and, hence, they are eager to use their skills to solve new questions and information problems.

In the Ending Stage of research, the primary information skills required are:

◆ **Presentation**: results are communicated via a presentation or report.

◆ **Evaluation**: the product and process are evaluated and methods for improvement are identified.

Now we return to the Motivation Overlay for Information Skills Instruction and move from the During Stage presented in Chapter Three to the final stage of the research process. In this chapter, we will complete the Motivation Toolkit, that is, the *start-up toolkit*. We fully expect that your Toolkit will include many more techniques and unique examples as you put your motivation skills to work. In fact, you may happily discover that your Toolkit actually *never* is completed, as you are forever adding brand-new ideas to it.

By the end of Chapter Four, you will:

◆ understand several key motivational goals that are applicable to the Ending Stage of the research process, in which students present their final work and evaluate both the work itself and the process used to achieve the final outcome

◆ be able to suggest motivational techniques that can be used to address motivational goals for a given situation in the Ending Stage of research

Kuhlthau's (1991) research shows that students experience a sense of relief as they approach the end of a research endeavor. However, this relief may be accompanied by a sense of accomplishment for some students and a sense of dissatisfaction and disappointment for others. Consequently, applying the Motivation

Overlay to information skills instruction at the Ending Stage is just as important as in the earlier stages.

Presentation, the first of the Ending Stage information skills, involves the communication of the students' research results in the form of a presentation or product. There are any number of formats this may take, such as:

◆ oral (individual or team) report

◆ written report

◆ computer-based report

◆ interactive multimedia

◆ graphic or other primarily visual display

◆ videotape

There are also a number of different forums for presentation in addition to the library media center or classroom. Forums may include live presentations in front of small or large groups or at special events; others include broadcast or cable television and, of course, the Internet. The format and forum of the presentation may also be influenced by the purpose of the presentation. For example, if the purpose includes an emotional plea to take action to decrease teenage drinking, then a videotape depicting the potentially violent consequences would be more persuasive than a written report alone.

The amount of time allocated to the various information skills in each stage of research also may vary. The duration may be for one class activity, a two-week assignment, a semester-long project, or perhaps even several years in a curriculum in which you focus on one or more skills in a particular year.

The final information skill, evaluation, is a critical (but often overlooked) part of the research process. Kuhlthau emphasizes the need for students to objectively assess their research activities at this stage. Stripling and Pitts's (1988) Research Process Model includes reflection points to assess one's progress throughout the process. (You may have noticed that we have included reflection points at the end of each chapter of this book to allow you to contemplate what you have read and jot down related thoughts and ideas.)

In their Big Six Model of Information Problem-Solving, Eisenberg and Berkowitz (1990) define evaluation in terms of both the product and the process.

The student evaluates whether his or her final *product* really answered the original question or definition of the problem—or how "effective" the product is. In addition, the student evaluates the *process* used to get to the final product and how "efficient" he or she was in carrying out all of the information skills involved.

While students' work may ultimately be evaluated by the teacher and/or LMS, it is important to encourage students to evaluate themselves as well. An opportunity to reflect on one's effort (process) and results (product) helps students to hone their information skills and become more self-determining researchers. We'll discuss self-evaluation further later in the chapter.

But what about students who are not successful in their research task? For these students, evaluation becomes even more crucial, with the teacher and/or LMS providing support and encouragement by helping the student identify what went wrong, guiding the student's attribution to either (lack of) effort or ability (lack of critical skills or knowledge), and identifying specific methods for improvement and strategies for future success. It is unlikely that these students will improve their performance to any great extent if this is not done.

The last part of the Motivation Overlay, as shown below, identifies the key motivational goals we will address for the Ending Stage of research. We begin with Goal #1: **Encourage ongoing confidence in students' research abilities**.

Figure 4-1. Motivational Goal #1: Ending Stage

Research Stages	Ending
Information Skills	Presentation Evaluation
Motivational Goals	✓ **Encourage ongoing confidence in research abilities** Promote satisfaction in research accomplishments Motivate continuing information exploration
Related Motivational Theories	Expectancy-value Curiosity Attribution Social learning

The major technique for accomplishing this goal is:

◆ tying learning success to effort

A number of strategies for implementing that technique are described in the following section of this chapter.

Encouraging Ongoing Confidence in Research Abilities

Once you have helped students develop confidence in their ability to research a topic and solve an information problem, you want to ensure that this confidence carries over to future research assignments. One of the most effective techniques to encourage ongoing confidence in research abilities is to *tie the student's successful completion of a research project to his or her own effort and ability* (i.e., knowledge and skills). According to the attribution theory discussed in Chapter One, a student who attributes his or her success to personal effort is more likely to succeed on the next project. Why? Because the student perceives that he or she can exercise control over the situation. A perception of control in turn increases one's expectation for success. If, on the other hand, the student perceives he or she was simply "lucky" (or "unlucky"), the chances for increased effort on the next occasion are lessened (along with the expectation for success).

What about students who did poorly? Try to help them recognize that more effort on their part would have made a difference. Avoid letting these students blame their lack of success on either luck or task difficulty. However, if a student actually did try and still did poorly, it may in fact be due to ability. The teacher or LMS may need to provide additional help and guidance to bring that student up to par with the rest of the class. Praise the effort and assure the student that with a little more help he or she will succeed.

A wonderful strategy for encouraging ongoing confidence is to provide opportunities for students who do well on a research assignment to peer-tutor other students on new assignments. Each could act as a kind of "coach" for one or more students. This strategy is beneficial to both the student who is tutoring and the student being tutored, in a number of ways.

For the peer tutor, teaching someone else something you have learned is one of the highest forms of learning and promises greater retention. It also helps encourage the peer tutor's continuing confidence in his/her research abilities. Furthermore, it is an excellent outlet for a peer tutor who is high in need for power because it is likely to have a meaningful impact on others.

For the student being tutored, it provides another source of help when the student is confused or falling behind. Relevance is also increased by observing a peer as a role model, especially if the peer tutor models enthusiasm for the task. You may recall that observation and modeling desirable behaviors is a strategy suggested by Bandura's (1997) social learning theory.

Peer-tutoring does not have to be reserved to teaching information skills only. LMS Kathy Spitzer and her colleagues at North Syracuse (New York) High School focus on fun ways to capture an audience and promote reading at the secondary level with a program called "Promoting Reading Peers." The librarians team up with the English Department to promote a book (in this particular case, *Dakota Dream*) that should be of interest to the target group. They purchase about 20 copies of the book and circulate it to as many readers (teachers and students) as possible within a period of four to five weeks. Following this, they invite all those who read the book to a lunchtime discussion of it, providing pizza or subs to facilitate the discussion. To spice things up they even create a few "extras," as Kathy describes: "We created a Hyperstudio slide show to enhance the discussion. We featured Native Americans and played Native American drum music while the slide show was going on."

The lunchtime discussion and activities made those who read the book feel good about their accomplishments and served as a kind of information reward for those who made the effort to read the book. This type of activity may also serve as a kind of catalyst for the same students to become unofficial peer tutors to those who have not yet read the book. In effect, they become promoters of the book as well.

Nelson (1994) recommends three guidelines for effective rewards in the workplace that are equally applicable to the classroom or library media. They are:

◆ Being timely and specific: as soon as possible after the desired behavior and explaining why the reward is given.

◆ Matching the reward to the person: the reward chosen is one that is valued by that individual.

◆ Matching the reward to the achievement: when a reward is tied to the successfully completed task (as opposed to being totally unrelated to the task). This also boosts confidence. For example, as described in Chapter One, a pizza party after completion of a research project would be fun, but a field trip to a place related to the research topic would be more relevant. The latter reward provides additional learning relevant to the task while the pizza party, alone, is more of a "controlling" reward. (However, Brophy [1998] warns that rewards are only effective motivators if students believe that if they put forth a reasonable amount of effort, they have a chance to get the reward.)

Deci (1995) identifies two types of rewards: those meant to control (e.g., "Finish this worksheet and you will be able to go to recess") and those that provide meaningful information and are tied to effort (e.g., "You can now join the 'Young Researchers Club' because you have worked hard and mastered the research process"). A controlling reward encourages students to engage in desired behaviors in order to achieve the reward and often undermines motivation tied to the learning by making the reward the end, rather than the means to the end. The more controlling the reward, the more likely it will decrease existing intrinsic motivation. The more informational the reward, the more likely it will increase feelings of competence and self-determination and enhance existing intrinsic motivation.

There are many types of tangible rewards that we give in schools—gold stars, parties, candy bars, prizes, grades, diplomas, etc. There are also intangible rewards that can be just as, or even more, effective motivators, such as recognition, promotion, control, freedom, opportunities, encouragement, and praise. Nelson (1994) reports that recognition of a job well done is the most powerful motivator of employee performance. We believe that recognition and praise can be equally powerful motivators of student performance.

Praise is an effective way of tying success to effort. Praise is perhaps the easiest and most common reward strategy but must only be given when deserved, and works best when accompanied by an explanation of why the student succeeded. Here is an example: "You did a great job on your report, Jimmy, because you took the time to identify some of the best sources on your topic!" In this example, success was tied directly to the student's effort.

Noncontrolling praise (e.g., "You did a great job!") helps enhance existing intrinsic motivation, while controlling praise that puts pressure on the student (e.g., "You did it just the way you were supposed to!") tends to diminish a child's intrinsic motivation (Deci, 1995). When examining the types of motivators used by elementary and middle school LMSs, Small found that 90% of the praise statements used by LMSs were informational and noncontrolling in nature (e.g., "Great! You seem to really remember how to do a bibliography"), as compared to only 10% controlling ("I'm going to tell Mrs. B. [classroom teacher] you get something from her candy jar").

It also may be that a student puts forth more effort if enthused about a topic, so you could also praise students for their enthusiasm. For example, "Your project, Maria, was one of the best in the class and I think it's because you liked your topic so much." If a student uses a novel approach to solve an information problem, you could praise his creativity. An example of this kind of praise is "I like the way you brought your own unique perspective to this project, Dan; it added so much more interest." All these techniques and examples serve to encourage students' ongoing confidence as young researchers.

Can you believe you are on the home stretch of developing your Motivation Toolkit? Below you will find the first goal, technique, and example strategies for the Ending section of your Toolkit.

Figure 4-2. Motivation Toolkit Goal #1: Ending Stage

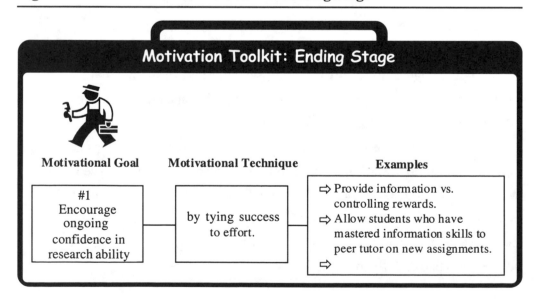

Encouraging ongoing confidence in research abilities is naturally an important aspect of E-V theory. It addresses the expectation-for-success component. Promoting satisfaction in research accomplishments, the next motivational goal in the Motivation Overlay, is key to both expectation for success *and* value. Students place a higher value on what provides them with a sense of satisfaction. We now turn our attention to Goal #2 in the Ending Stage: **to promote satisfaction in research accomplishments**.

Figure 4-3. Motivational Goal #2: Ending Stage

Research Stages	Ending
Information Skills	Presentation Evaluation
Motivational Goals	Encourage ongoing confidence in research abilities ✓ **Promote satisfaction in research accomplishments** Motivate continuing information exploration
Related Motivational Theories	Expectancy-value Curiosity Attribution Social learning

We suggest the following three techniques to achieve this goal:

◆ reflecting on learning success

◆ providing recognition or rewards for learning progress and success

◆ providing opportunities for self-assessment

We also suggest several motivational strategies to implement each of these broader techniques.

Promoting Satisfaction in Research Accomplishments

One way to promote satisfaction in one's research accomplishments is to give students the opportunity to *reflect on their research successes* —from their initial feelings when the project started all the way to the present moment. Based on our practical experience working with kids and based on Kuhlthau's (1991) work describing students in the research process, we can almost guarantee you'll get an earful. While some students may expound on the confusion they felt early on, you will want to help them recall the moments when things felt like they were really coming together. For example, a successful search strategy may have led to some interesting but surprising information. Other students may have become so absorbed when they started actually exploring for information that they lost track of time and space (a flow experience). Still others may have felt a curious sense of power after mastering an online searching technique. The point is that reflecting on one's experience helps to demonstrate just how far one has progressed.

Following this type of reflection, it becomes easier to reinforce the *intrinsic* value of learning information skills. Grades aside, it simply feels great to achieve mastery. No one, including adults, wants to fail. Harvey Miller, owner of Quill Corporation, once said, "It's a company's responsibility to allow each individual to be as good as he or she is capable of being. People basically want to do a good job. I never heard anybody walk out of this building and say, 'Boy, I feel great! I did a lousy job today'" (1988).

Another way to reflect on one's learning progress is through the use of portfolios. Portfolios are "a collection of a student's work which can be used to demonstrate his or her skills and accomplishments" (Lankes, 1995). Students can create what Lankes calls a "developmental portfolio," which can be used for reflecting on the successes of a learning experience and evaluation. (For another excellent description of the use of portfolios, see Crockett, 1998.)

The next Motivational Moment is a terrific one and an excellent example of the wonderful things that can happen when LMSs and classroom teachers team up on projects. Although we will focus on the presentation and evaluation aspects in the actual Motivational Moment, it will be necessary to describe LMS Pam Tinker's whole project to make sense of the Ending Stage motivational goals. So here goes.

Pam and the third grade teacher worked together to plan an implement a lesson in which students learn about technology while studying biomes (e.g., deserts, rainforests, tundra, etc.). The students were to create what they called a "Techno-Biome." Each student was placed in two groups, a "biome" group and a "home" group. Each was expected to become an "expert" on his or her assigned biome and bring that expertise to his or her home group. In this way, each home group was made up of an expert on each type of biome.

Pam and the third grade teacher began by having the entire class brainstorm what characteristics they wanted to know about each biome in order to generate a fill-in-the-blank chart with information such as what animals, plants, climate, and landforms are found in that biome. They agreed that before they sent the students off to create their own charts, they needed to practice with the students using one biome. So they created a chart with the desired information for a rainforest and created a shadow box of what that biome might look like using all the criteria they would have to use. This served as a model for the whole class.

Each biome group then went off to use the various resources in the library media center—CD-ROMs, the Internet, books—anything they could find to fill in their chart. They were told they had to create a picture of what they thought the biome would look like based on everything they had heard and read. Once each biome group had filled in their chart and created their picture, they then had to create a biome box (shadow box) that contained some of the plants and animals and other features of their biome.

After their biome boxes were completed, each student went back to his or her home group. Each home group, then, consisted of one student from each of the biome groups so that there was an expert on all of the biomes in each home group. Their next task was for each home group to create a "composite" animal, using recycled materials they brought from home and that Pam and the teacher had collected, that could live in all the biomes they had studied. Each biome expert had to make sure the animal could live in all the types of biome. Each animal was created to scale and put into a biome box.

Let's take a breather to reflect for a moment on this exciting project before we continue with its related Ending Stage Motivational Moment. As you probably realized, a number of motivational goals were addressed and strategies were employed in the Beginning and During Stages of this project concentrating on collection and organization skills. Since this chapter focuses on *Ending Stage* strategies, we'll just mention a couple of the strategies used and let you reflect on the others. What really stands out are the relevance and confidence-building strategies. They immediately build relevance through having the class brainstorm characteristics *they* (the students) would like to know about each biome. Brainstorming is a good participation technique that also helps to sustain attention. The confidence strategies incorporated a *practice* component before sending students off on their own and providing a fill-in-the-blank chart that served as a support or guidance tool while students were collecting information (students themselves helped to generate the chart—a *relevance* strategy). Since each biome group consisted of a number of students, each member of the group had the help of the others before returning to the home group where he or she would be the "sole expert," another excellent confidence-building strategy. Remember McClelland's (1961) Achievement Motivation Theory? Two motives are well served in this example. They are need for affiliation (teamwork) and need for power (the opportunity to be the "expert").

Now that you have the necessary background on this project, let's take a look at how this team handled the Ending Stage of research, consisting of presentation and evaluation, in the following Motivational Moment.

▶ Motivational Moment

Library Media Specialist:	**Pam Tinker**
School Name & Location:	Thorton's Ferry Elementary School, Merrimack, New Hampshire
Grade Level:	3
Instructional Goal:	To compare and contrast characteristics of different biomes
Information Skills:	Presentation, Evaluation
Motivational Goal:	To promote satisfaction in research accomplishments

The third grade classroom teacher and I had collaborated on a project on the characteristics of various biomes such as deserts, rainforests, and tundra. The students had a great time collecting and organizing the information prior to the presentation and evaluation phase of the project. Each student had acquired some expertise on his or her specific biome and reported the findings to the student's home group. That meant that each home group had several different "experts." The home group's task was then to create a composite animal that would be capable of living in all the biomes. Here is what we did for the presentation and evaluation tasks.

Each group prepared a multimedia slide show using ClarisWorks. We took digital pictures of each animal in its biome box. The students also created black line drawings with all the parts of each animal. We scanned those in and then added text describing how their animal was adapted to live in the particular biome. The students were very creative and some of the animals were pretty scary. They were also required to keep a bibliography of sources they used and to maintain a daily research journal containing notes, concept maps, and other reflections not only about what they had learned but also what they had discovered about the research process, themselves, and how they do research. For example, some found out they didn't work well in groups, while others preferred group work.

When they finished putting together their show, we invited parents and other classes to the library media center to see the presentations. Each group also talked about research and what they had learned about research. It was great because every student had to be an expert in something, so the brighter students had to make sure the slower students had all the information they needed to take back to their home group. That meant that every student contributed to his or her home group's research project. Some kids were more creative and did artwork; some focused on finding information from resources, etc. The teacher said it was one of the most successful units in her 20 years of teaching. The kids really had a great time with it!

Pam mentioned that the students were very creative. We think *Pam* was very creative, too! What a great motivator! The fact that the third grade teacher said it was one of the most successful units in all her years of teaching is the kind of response that will promote the concept of LMS/teacher collaboration.

Pam used excellent motivational techniques. She addressed both *format* and *forum* in terms of presentation. Students could express not only their knowledge but also their creativity using multimedia as the *format*. Since it was a group presentation, students could share the responsibility with different students working on aspects of the presentation that related to their individual strengths.

Beyond format, Pam and her counterpart selected a *forum* for the students' presentations in which students would garner recognition from both parents and peers. Both the format and forum for the presentation of this project addressed her motivational goal of *promoting satisfaction in research accomplishments*.

Students maintained a research journal, a valuable tool during the Ending Stage of research to help students hone their evaluation skills. The journal, which included additional strategies such as concept maps, aided students in reflecting upon both their final products (multimedia show) and the process they went through to get there. She notes that students discovered valuable insights into their own personal styles and individual differences as they relate to the research process (e.g., preferences for group vs. independent work). What additional comments would you add to debriefing Pam's Motivational Moment?

In Chapter Two, which focused on the Beginning Stage of research, we said that giving students a choice of research topics or formats helped to establish the importance of learning information skills by relating to the interest of students. Now, in the Ending Stage, allowing students to present their work in a variety of forums and then ***providing recognition or rewards for exemplary work*** will help promote students' satisfaction in their research accomplishments.

Debbie Stafford adapted a strategy, generously shared by a colleague through the Big 6 listserv, with great results in the following Motivational Moment.

▶ Motivational Moment

Library Media Specialist:	**Debbie Stafford**
School Name & Location:	Gen. H.H. Arnold High School, Wiesbaden, Germany
Grade Levels:	9-12
Instructional Goal:	To discover different lifestyle aspects of the Golden Age of Greece
Information Skill:	Presentation
Motivational Goal:	To promote satisfaction in research accomplishments

I worked with the teacher doing a unit on ancient Greece where we had students research different aspects of life in the Golden Age of Greece. I considered different presentation ideas like having a roundtable discussion or some sort of "Meet the Press" where students perform the role of the different people of the times as they have researched them. A newspaper or an interview program where students also do some role-playing would also work well. Ultimately, we did a *talk radio* show that featured interviews with people of the times. It included a sports report (based on the Olympics, of course), lifestyles, arts and entertainment, etc. The students really got into it.

In Debbie's Motivational Moment, it is likely that the final product, a talk radio show, became its own intrinsic reward because it was so much fun to do. Students probably also received recognition from their listening audience—the other students and teachers. You can also find alternative ways to have students present their research results. For example, producing brochures requires students to be succinct about the way they present the results of their research. They are also easy to display on a bulletin board to provide recognition to those students who do exemplary work.

Although we discussed variety as an effective technique for the During Stage of the research process, it is also appropriate for the Ending Stage, but in a different way. In the Ending Stage, variety pertains to the research product—not always using the same format (e.g., written report, oral presentation to class, etc.) or forum (classroom, public event, media, school event, etc.). Variety helps to increase motivation by maintaining interest and addressing student learning styles. While the written report may have seemed "old hat" and "boring" to the above students, the idea of creating a brochure for the final product was much more satisfying. Debbie concluded that the project is worthwhile and lends itself to different formats. Perhaps next year it could be a newspaper or interactive multimedia display.

One of the authors of this book created a unique forum as a culminating activity for demonstrating the results of a research project on censorship of library books. (The first part of this project was described in Chapter Three.) After investigating the censorship issue, the LMS invited an author of a young adult book that some communities had attempted to ban from libraries, an attorney, the president of the school board, and her school's principal to be on a panel to discuss the censorship issue. The students prepared questions and formed strong opinions as they went face-to-face with the panel and a lively debate ensued. The school's video club videotaped the event for parents and other students to watch at a later date. After the activity, the LMS held a debriefing session with students to evaluate the entire experience and their participation in it. Everyone felt it was an excellent learning experience that made them think in depth about all the issues involved and evaluate the quality of their participation.

Evaluation is one of the most important critical thinking skills for students to learn. Today, students must not only be capable of evaluating information and information resources (print, audiovisual, and electronic), but they must also learn to evaluate themselves in terms of the products they create and the processes they use when tapping into those vast information resources.

You may wish to share your own criteria for evaluating information products for students to use as guidelines for developing their own measures of self-evaluation. The grade for the project could even be a combination of teacher and student self-evaluation. *Providing opportunities for self-assessment* helps to keep the learner actively engaged in the learning process and may reveal new insights as well as new skills that the learner discovered during the process. In the next Motivational Moment, Mary-Elizabeth Rhoads and graduate intern Lauren Fitch used a questioning technique for students to evaluate their own and each other's presentations.

▶ Motivational Moment

Library Media Specialist: **Mary-Elizabeth Rhoads**
Graduate Student Intern: Lauren Fitch
School Name & Location: African Road Elementary School,
                            Vestal, New York

Grade Level: 5
Instructional Goal: To gain experience in public speaking and
                            using presentation technology
Information Skills: Presentation, Evaluation
Motivational Goal: To promote satisfaction in research
                            accomplishments

The fifth grade students were assigned to read a novel of their choice and put together a mini-Power Point presentation (three slides) about their novel, including promoting the book as if they were selling it, kind of a "mini-booktalk." The students scanned in pictures and learned many technical skills while finishing their projects—skills they would need when they moved on to middle school next year. We then put all the slide shows together into one presentation and presented it to the students. At that time, each student had to prepare questions about each of the other contributions and be prepared to answer questions about his or her own contribution. The questions ranged from why they did certain things (e.g., whether the background they chose was related to the story) to why they chose that particular book to why they said what they did to promote the book. This required the students to evaluate how and why they made decisions about what information to include and how they used the technology. This really gave them a chance to assess their work and the methods they used to create it. Afterwards, the children felt very satisfied about creating this electronic presentation because they (like Frank Sinatra) did it their way!

What satisfaction strategies did you find in the above Motivational Moment? Lauren and Mary-Elizabeth gave students choices and a good degree of freedom in the way in which these fifth graders presented and evaluated their projects. For example, while students were offered some guidance, they seemed to have plenty of latitude when creating their own mini-presentations. Such freedom of expression certainly promotes satisfaction about research accomplishments, as does the opportunity to make up one's own questions for evaluating others' research. Each student also had the opportunity to see how his or her *part* contributed to the *whole,* which is very rewarding as well.

The assessment activity focused on the final product *and* the process used to create it, without detracting from the individual creativity each student brought to the project. Questioning (particularly from peers) was an excellent way to stimulate students' self-assessment, making them look at their work more objectively, which Donham (1998) calls "an important skill for lifelong learning" (p. 222).

There are many other ways to help students evaluate their research products and process. Anne Croak, currently co-director of curriculum and technology at the Medfield Public Schools, shared this experience she had as an elementary LMS. Anne used brainstorming at the end of a project as an informal way to help students evaluate the process they went through in this Motivational Moment.

▶ Motivational Moment

Library Media Specialist:	**Anne Lawless Croak**
School Name & Location:	T.A. Blake Middle School, Medford, Massachusetts
Grade Level:	6
Instructional Goal:	To determine ways to improve research outcomes
Information Skill:	Evaluation
Motivational Goal:	To promote satisfaction in research accomplishments

I was the new LMS in a middle school building and a teacher brought her class to the library to do a research project on Greek gods and goddesses. Since I was new and still learning the ropes, this was a project she had done many years in a row, and was a project that the kids enjoyed, I just followed her lead, letting her set up the project the way she wanted.

What I did was wait until the project was over and then brainstorm with the kids about the process they had used. I asked questions like What was the task you were asked to accomplish? What resources could you have used? How did you decide which resources, and where were they? How did you find the information within them? How did you get/record information from them? What did you make to show what you learned? How did you know if you did your job well? How will you do similar projects when they are assigned? What might you do differently? We really analyzed the project afterwards and I could then explain that what they had really done was use something called Big 6. Talk about teaching library skills in context and making sense to sixth graders!

By getting students involved in brainstorming as a means of self-assessment, Anne increased relevance by eliciting feedback from the students themselves. Brainstorming also gives students a chance to vent if they are unhappy with the project. This, in turn, helps an LMS when doing a Motivational Makeover! We have summarized Goal #2 with suggested techniques and examples in the following part of the Motivation Toolkit.

Figure 4-4. Motivation Toolkit Goal #2: Ending Stage

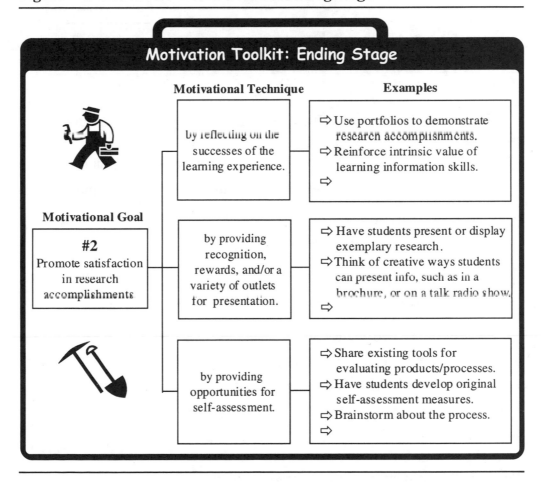

Motivation Toolkit: Ending Stage

	Motivational Technique	**Examples**
	by reflecting on the successes of the learning experience.	⇨ Use portfolios to demonstrate research accomplishments. ⇨ Reinforce intrinsic value of learning information skills. ⇨
Motivational Goal **#2** Promote satisfaction in research accomplishments	by providing recognition, rewards, and/or a variety of outlets for presentation.	⇨ Have students present or display exemplary research. ⇨ Think of creative ways students can present info, such as in a brochure, or on a talk radio show. ⇨
	by providing opportunities for self-assessment.	⇨ Share existing tools for evaluating products/processes. ⇨ Have students develop original self-assessment measures. ⇨ Brainstorm about the process. ⇨

Perhaps the greatest achievement by an educator is to motivate students to want to *continue* to explore and learn—to create what *Information Power* (AASL and AECT, 1998) calls "a community of lifelong learners" (p. vii)—even when incentives such as grades or rewards are removed. We have now reached the final goal of the Motivation Overlay's Ending Stage: **to motivate students to continue information exploration**.

Figure 4-5. Motivational Goal #3: Ending Stage

Research Stages	Ending
Information Skills	Presentation Evaluation
Motivational Goals	Encourage ongoing confidence in research abilities Promote satisfaction in research accomplishments ✓ **Motivate continuing information exploration**
Related Motivational Theories	Expectancy-value Curiosity Attribution Social learning

We've identified two motivational techniques related to this last Motivation Goal:

◆ providing enrichment opportunities

◆ offering new opportunities for applying information skills

Several motivational strategies related to each of the above techniques are also described.

Motivating Continuing Information Exploration

Because of the importance of developing a positive attitude toward lifelong learning, we consider the last goal to be the most important motivationally. Naturally, there is a greater chance of achieving this goal given success in achieving the prior goals. One effective strategy for motivating continuing information exploration is *providing enrichment opportunities* that will engage the learner after the project or assignment is completed. Enrichment could take the form of additional reading, allowing students to use more sophisticated research tools, or opportunities to present results to new audiences. Sometimes, enrichment opportunities happen quite unexpectedly, as we see in the next Motivational Moment.

▶ **Motivational Moment**

Enrichment Teacher:	**Anna Waldron**
School Name & Location:	Lansing Middle School, Lansing, New York
Grade Level:	5
Instructional Goal:	To research additional information about Halley's Comet
Information Skills:	Exploration, Collection, Presentation
Motivational Goal:	To motivate continuing information exploration

A group of fifth graders was creating a play. The play had to be based on a historic event set in the Middle Ages. The students knew about knights and castles, but they weren't familiar with any events except for the legendary King Arthur and his travels. We decided that since the King Arthur legend has so many versions, it would be best to find another person or event on which to base the play.

The students looked on the Internet for information about the Middle Ages. Using WebTV, they searched for "Middle Ages." After perusing some websites, they found a time line of the Middle Ages and decided to use the event in 1066 when Halley's Comet passed the Earth. The students were so excited about the event (they had heard about the comet in science class) that I decided to give them an opportunity for enrichment. Their task was to go to the school or public library before our next class (two days) and bring to class some additional information on Halley's Comet. Two days later, every student remembered to bring his or her information to class. We had books, websites, and newspaper and magazine articles. They couldn't wait to share the information with each other and me. We learned historic, scientific, and literary information related to Halley's Comet. The students went above and beyond what I expected, and we gained knowledge that we never would have had time to learn in class. It was truly a motivational moment!

During the course of a research assignment on the Middle Ages, Anna capitalized on serendipity, when the students showed intrinsic curiosity about a related topic, Halley's Comet. With just a little bit of direction, Anna sent the students off to explore information and gather resources. Student interest provided value, and the information skills they had developed provided the expectation for success at the task. We think you'll agree that this experience was highly satisfying for both Anna and her students.

Anna's Motivational Moment could also be used to illustrate a second method for motivating continuing information exploration. Once students have gained competence as information problem solvers, ***offer new opportunities for applying information skills*** to a new context. Remember how important curiosity was in generating interest in the research process in the Beginning Stage? It is *still* important in the Ending Stage of the research process. By stimulating student curiosity in a new or related question or information problem, we help to motivate continuing information exploration even after the research project is completed. This may happen unexpectedly (as in Anna's situation) or may be planned, based on the information we gather about students' needs and interests for our motivational profiles. Exploration may be pursued outside of school—something of personal interest a student chooses to explore independently, confident that he or she possesses the requisite information skills to be successful.

Expectancy-value theory, therefore, comes into play once more as we examine students who choose to continue to explore for information even after the task is completed. Those are the students who see the *value* in both the research skills and the topic to be researched, and have the *expectation that they have the knowledge and skills to be successful* in their research. Celebrate when you see such students because this is confirmation that you have succeeded in your task: motivating your students to become truly information literate.

Finally, we have come to the last part of your Motivation Toolkit! Remember, we've left some empty spaces for you to fill in your own ideas for customizing your Toolkit.

Figure 4-6. Motivation Toolkit Goal #3: Ending Stage

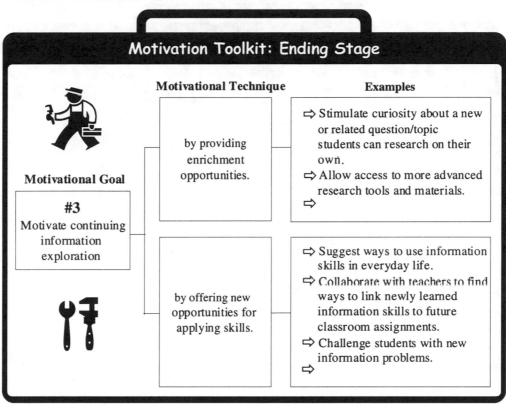

On the next page, we have compiled all three goals in the Ending Stage of the research process.

Figure 4-7. Motivation Toolkit: Ending Stage

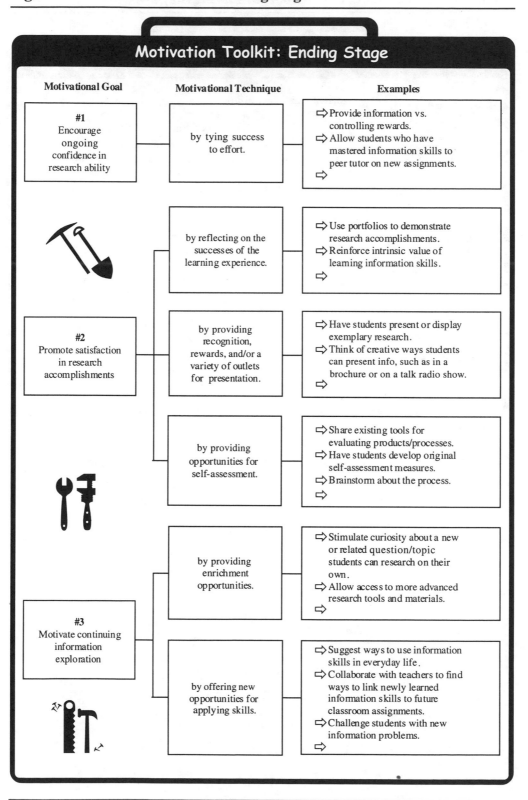

Motivation Toolkit: Ending Stage

Motivational Goal	Motivational Technique	Examples
#1 Encourage ongoing confidence in research ability	by tying success to effort.	⇨ Provide information vs. controlling rewards. ⇨ Allow students who have mastered information skills to peer tutor on new assignments. ⇨
#2 Promote satisfaction in research accomplishments	by reflecting on the successes of the learning experience.	⇨ Use portfolios to demonstrate research accomplishments. ⇨ Reinforce intrinsic value of learning information skills. ⇨
	by providing recognition, rewards, and/or a variety of outlets for presentation.	⇨ Have students present or display exemplary research. ⇨ Think of creative ways students can present info, such as in a brochure or on a talk radio show. ⇨
	by providing opportunities for self-assessment.	⇨ Share existing tools for evaluating products/processes. ⇨ Have students develop original self-assessment measures. ⇨ Brainstorm about the process. ⇨
#3 Motivate continuing information exploration	by providing enrichment opportunities.	⇨ Stimulate curiosity about a new or related question/topic students can research on their own. ⇨ Allow access to more advanced research tools and materials. ⇨
	by offering new opportunities for applying skills.	⇨ Suggest ways to use information skills in everyday life. ⇨ Collaborate with teachers to find ways to link newly learned information skills to future classroom assignments. ⇨ Challenge students with new information problems. ⇨

What Would YOU Do?

?

You just completed the research project that the fourth grade science students have been working on all term. One student, Jamal, who showed little interest at the beginning of the research project, suddenly became excited toward the end when he turned up an interesting incidental fact about Neanderthal man that got him thinking. He didn't have the time to carry it through so he finished up his project on the less interesting topic he chose at the beginning of the term. You wonder if there is any way that you can motivate Jamal to continue researching this side topic on his own. **What would you do?**

!

Jamal needed to find something interesting before he could become fully invested in the research project. Unfortunately, he found the catalyst for his interest a bit late in the term. Finally, his curiosity was piqued. You know you have an opportunity to stimulate his curiosity and motivate him to use his research skills, if only there were a way to make it work. You realize he didn't get the grade he had hoped for on the project, so perhaps there is a way to use both extrinsic and intrinsic satisfaction strategies to get Jamal motivated to continue an information search. You might try talking to the science teacher and asking if it would be possible for Jamal to do a special research assignment for extra credit.

Motivational Makeover

Are you ready for one last lackluster lesson plan? (How's that for alliteration?) This plan was submitted by Susan Limpert, who was acting LMS at a small urban K-5 school. In between the *before* and *after* plans, we include Susan's own debriefing of what went awry and what went well the first time around. Her Lackluster Lesson Plan appears on the next page.

▶ **Lackluster Lesson Plan**

Audience: Third and fourth graders

Topic: Using the encyclopedia

Instructional Goal: To introduce students to using the encyclopedia

Informational Skill: Exploration

Procedures:

Day 1

1. Raise a relevant, interesting question from a story read to the class.

2. Show how quickly and easily it can be answered using the encyclopedia.

Day 2

3. Rave about the encyclopedias. Flip through a volume and show the students all the colorful pictures. Discuss some of the different kinds of information you can find in the encyclopedia. Read some things of interest to third and fourth graders.

4. Give time for students to look through an encyclopedia volume. Tell them to "show me something cool." Show them what I mean while they are looking.

Day 3

5. Tell students that there is going to be an information scavenger hunt using the encyclopedias and there will be a prize.

6. Discuss how the encyclopedia is organized alphabetically.

7. Have the students pair up. Give them the question sheets and assign them to a volume of the encyclopedia. Explain that the word they need to look up to answer the question is in bold print and the answer to the question is in the first couple of lines of the entry. Tell them that their teacher and I will be available to help them.

8. Everyone who finishes gets "Smarties" (because they are smarties).

Susan critiqued her own lesson plan before doing her motivational makeover. She started with things that worked.

"Parts of this lesson actually went over quite well. Unconsciously, I had used some motivational techniques. I used relevance when I used the encyclopedia to answer a question we came up with in class and when I modeled enthusiasm for the activity. From Bandura's Social Learning Model (1997), their teacher and I used modeling of the desired behaviors when we did step 4 with the students. I considered some students' affiliation motive from McClelland's Achievement Motivation Theory (1961) when I had them work in groups of two (actually, I ran out of time making up the question sheets)."

Then she discussed what she felt were the problem areas in her initial lesson plan.

"From what I learned in the seminar, I can see that my lesson had no overall relevance. I should have planned with the teacher ahead of time so that the students' use of the encyclopedias tied in with something they were studying in class. Also, my use of an extrinsic reward was not effective. It actually caused the students to work in a frenzy for the prize. They did not really think about the questions or what they were doing. They just wanted to do it fast and get help fast. The other problem that shocked me was that most of the students could not find the words or the answers (especially since I thought I had made it so simple). Because I knew that they had to alphabetize their weekly spelling words, I assumed that they had the skill of looking up words in alphabetical order. I did not know my audience well enough!"

After analyzing her audience a bit more, Susan fine-tuned her lesson plan. You'll also notice that she modified the instructional goal somewhat and really worked to increase relevance. Now, let's take a look at her Motivational Makeover. It begins on the next page.

▶ Susan's Motivational Makeover

Audience: 24 third and fourth graders with skills about a grade below

Topic: Trip Around the World

Instructional Goal: To gain a basic awareness of countries around the world (from fourth grade curriculum)

Information Skills: Definition, Exploration, Collection, Presentation

Motivational Goals: To generate interest in the research process. To establish the importance of information skills. To build confidence in research ability.

Motivational Measures: Observed excitement. Time on task. Enthusiasm for results.

Lesson Plan:

1. Tell the students that we are going to take an imaginary trip around the world. We need to decide where we are going to go and what we want to see there. As a class, we are going to put together our trip itinerary. Show example of itinerary. One student will be our tour guide for each country we will visit. Their performance will be part of their Social Studies grade.

2. Spin the globe and have each student come up and pick a country at random. Let them put a sticker with their name on it on the world map. The student reports will go in the order of the route we would travel from Syracuse.

3. Brainstorm what information we want to know about our destinations.

4. Tell them that we will use the encyclopedias to find this information. Show them an example of a country entry in the encyclopedia. Show them that they can get some ideas from the pictures. Tell them which parts of the entry they should read and take notes on.

5. Give them plenty of time to use the encyclopedias. Walk around the room and give feedback to each student as he or she works.

6. Reconvene as a group and have each student tell one interesting thing he or she discovered about their topic.

7. Explain that during the next class we will use the computers to make up our class itinerary.

Susan's lesson is an example of compressing a number of information skills into a mini-project covering a short span of time. Thus, she also addresses one or more of the Motivational Goals from the Beginning, During, and Ending Stages of research. Telling the students about the imaginary trip around the world will help to generate interest in the research process by creating positive anticipation with her unique approach. Curiosity can be aroused as she spins the globe and gives each child a chance to pick a country at random. Relevance is increased by having each student become the tour guide for the country he or she selects. Susan also addresses the importance of the research task by tying it to part of their Social Studies grade. By allowing enough *time* to use the encyclopedias, she helps to build student confidence and lessen potential anxiety about research. By providing feedback to individual students while they are exploring and collecting information, she will help to reinforce their confidence in their research ability. Finally, she promotes satisfaction in their research accomplishments when, upon reconvening, she has each student in a group tell something interesting he or she discovered about the topic.

What do you think of Susan's plan? Will her motivational techniques work? Can you use any of her ideas for your own instruction?

▶ Chapter Challenge

1. How many different formats for presenting research can you think of? Try to come up with a few more not mentioned in this chapter.

2. What forums for presentation might be available at your school or in your community?

3. Which information problem-solving model emphasizes the evaluation of both the research product and the research process?

4. Why is it that a student who attributes his or her success to personal effort is more likely to succeed on the next project?

5. What is an often-used means of helping students reflect on their learning progress by collecting assignments and other evidence over time?

6. What should you do about a student who put forth a good effort on a research project but still did poorly?

7. Think back to McClelland's (1961) Theory of Achievement Motivation. Which of his three motives does peer-tutoring most closely address? Is there another of his motives that it could also address?

8. What are two techniques that can be used to motivate continuing information exploration?

9. Stimulating curiosity is important in the Beginning Stage of research. Why is it also important in the Ending Stage?

10. How does E-V theory help to explain students who continue to explore even after the research project is completed?

▶ Chapter Challenge: Answers

1. Examples are oral (individual or team) reports, written reports, computer-based presentations (e.g., Power Point), interactive multimedia (e.g., Hyperstudio), graphic or visual display, videotape.

2. Examples could include school newspaper, local newspaper, local television or cable station, school or local radio station, school or community special event.

3. Big Six Information Problem-Solving Model (Eisenberg and Berkowitz, 1990).

4. Because the student has a sense of personal control over the outcome.

5. Creating a portfolio.

6. Praise the effort, offer extra help and support, and continue to build confidence.

7. Need for power because it allows one student to influence another. May also appeal to need for affiliation because it requires working with others.

8. Providing enrichment opportunities and offering new opportunities for applying skills.

9. In the Beginning Stage, stimulating curiosity helps to generate interest in the research process; in the Ending Stage it helps to motivate continuing information exploration even after the research project is completed.

10. E-V theory helps to identify which students might choose to continue to explore for information even after the task is completed. They are the students who have discovered the *value* of information skills and the topic they wish to explore, and have the *expectation that they can be successful* in their research efforts.

Reflection Points

Please use this page to record your ideas and special points to remember from Chapter Four.

References

AASL and AECT, *Information Power: Building Partnerships for Learning* (Chicago: American Library Association, 1998).

Bandura, Albert, *Social Learning Theory* (Englewood Cliffs, NJ: Prentice-Hall, 1977).

Brophy, Jere, *Motivating Students to Learn* (Boston, MA: McGraw-Hill, 1998).

Crockett, Tom, *The Portfolio Journey: A Creative Guide to Keeping Student-Managed Portfolios in the Classroom* (Englewood, CO: Teacher Ideas Press, 1998).

Deci., E. L., *Why We Do What We Do: Understanding Self-Motivation* (New York: Penguin Books, 1995).

Donham, Jean, *Enhancing Teaching and Learning: A Leadership Guide for School Library Media Specialists* (New York: Neal-Schuman, 1998).

Eisenberg, Michael E., and Robert E. Berkowitz, *Information Problem-Solving: The Big Six Approach to Library and Information Skills Instruction* (Norwood, NJ: Ablex, 1990).

Hanks, Kurt, *Motivating People: How to Motivate Others to Do What You Want and Thank You for the Opportunity* (Menlo Park, CA: Crisp Publications, 1991).

Kuhlthau, Carol, "Inside the Search Process: Information Seeking from the User's Perspective," *Journal of the American Society of Information Science* 42, no. 5 (1991): 361-71.

Lankes, Anna Maria D., "Electronic Portfolios: A New Idea in Assessment," *ERIC Digest* (Dec. 1995).

Lowenthal, Barbara, "The Power of Suggestion," *Academic Therapy* 21 (1986): 537-41.

McClelland, David C., *The Achieving Society* (New York: Wiley, 1961).

Miller, Harvey, *Nation's Business* (Mar. 1988).

Nelson, Bob, *1001 Ways to Reward Employees* (New York: Workman Publishing, 1994).

Stripling, Barbara K., and Judy Pitts, *Brainstorms and Blueprints: Teaching Library Research as a Thinking Process* (Englewood, CO: Libraries Unlimited, 1988).

Wlodkowski, Raymond, *Enhancing Adult Motivation to Learn: A Guide to Improving Instruction and Increasing Learner Achievement* (San Francisco, CA: Jossey-Bass, 1993).

Chapter Five

Putting It All Together

> ❝ When truth is seen as a process of construction in which the knower participates, a passion for learning is unleashed. ❞
>
> ~ Belenky et al., 1986, p.140

Introduction

Now that you have seen the entire Motivation Overlay for Information Skills Instruction and constructed a Motivation Toolkit, we would like to pull it all together by revisiting the Scenario presented in Chapter One, reviewing some of the key points made throughout this book, and begining to explore the relationship of motivation and information literacy to constructivist learning environments. We believe information literacy thrives in constructivist learning environments because of its goal to empower students as "independent users of ideas and information." By the end of Chapter Five, you will:

- ◆ be able to apply motivational principles and techniques described in previous chapters to the Scenario presented in Chapter One
- ◆ understand the role of the Motivation Overlay for Information Skills Instruction in constructivist learning environments
- ◆ be able to apply motivational principles and techniques to new instructional challenges

Remember poor Sam Downey, the high school LMS in our Chapter One Scenario? He was faced with a crisis that was full of danger—but also one that offered a wonderful opportunity for Sam to make a difference in the lives of his students. Before you read some of our suggestions for Sam, you may want to reread the Scenario and think about some ways Sam could have prevented the situation he found himself in and other ways in which he could improve this situation. Which of the following types of strategies do you think Sam is most in need of incorporating into his lesson?

- ◆ strategies to increase the confidence of his students to successfully complete research tasks
- ◆ strategies for generating interest and curiosity in research tasks
- ◆ strategies that illustrate the value of acquiring information skills

We presented Sam's dilemma to some practitioners in the field and asked them what they thought Sam could have done better or differently. We've incorporated their ideas with some of our own and present them here.

Scenario Revisited

The approach that Sam took set him up for problems with this class from the very beginning. First of all, Sam could have developed a motivational profile of this class in order to be better prepared. The fact that these students were new should have shed some light on their potential motivational profile. New students often bring with them a level of anxiety that could have been manifested in some of the behaviors noted. This could have suggested to Sam that he start with motivational techniques that would break the ice and possibly create positive anticipation for the learning, thus reducing initial anxiety while capturing their attention.

He could then utilize strategies that would stimulate their curiosity and interest. For example, Sam could have had large, odd-shaped posters on the walls with thought-provoking questions on each poster. He also could have shared some "inside information"—that over the years this first session with students seems to always predict how well they will do with the research projects they encounter during the year—alerting students to the importance of what will be covered in the session.

A motivational profile might also have uncovered the less than positive past research experiences of some students, which would have alerted Sam to the immediate need for building students' confidence in their research ability. For this, Sam must create a supportive learning environment in which students believe they can succeed. He also needed to establish a rapport with his students. For example, on that first day (and until Sam got to know the students) both he and the students could wear name tags so they could call each other by name. This strategy usually facilitates rapport-building, generates more positive interactions, and cuts down on inappropriate talking and other acting-out behaviors.

Did you notice Sam's enthusiasm at the beginning of the lesson—or should we say *lack* of enthusiasm? Sam's tone and manner did nothing to excite his students about what they were about to learn—in fact, just the opposite. Basically, he seemed to just want to get through the period (i.e., he had a lot of information and only 30 minutes to cram it into them). If Sam had modeled more of a sense of excitement about the research process, he might have ignited a spark in his students.

Once he had their attention, Sam needed to establish the importance of information skills in their lives. He could have started the lesson by asking students about times outside of school when they had to find information to solve a problem in their lives, and what helped them and what hindered them in their search. In this way, Sam could build on their existing knowledge and prepare them for more difficult learning in a nonthreatening way. This would also help prevent students who had had less than positive past research experiences from being immediately intimidated by launching right into an information problem-solving model, helping to build their research self-confidence and a more internal attribution for their outcomes.

Sam could then tell the students that, although they may not have realized it, they were solving their information problem by using an information problem-solving model. At this point, Sam could show students the pieces of a colorful poster (representing the parts of an information problem-solving model that is cut up like a jigsaw puzzle). He could tell them he had this great poster but somehow it ended up in pieces, maintaining their interest by sustaining curiosity and providing an element of mystery.

As Sam calls on individual students to help him fit the pieces into the puzzle (each piece could have adhesive on the back so that it can be put up on the wall or bulletin board), he could ask them how each of these information skills was used in their information problem example, thereby promoting inquiry and participation, relating back to their personal needs, and showing them the usefulness of information skills in their own daily lives. He could use this opportunity to fully describe each skill, clarify any inaccurate perceptions, and acknowledge the anxiety and uncertainty they may feel at various points in the process, reinforcing the development of their research self-confidence.

Sam could also take a minute or two to relate one or more personal stories of using an information problem-solving model to solve his own information problems, thereby promoting the value of learning information skills. He might even mention some of the anxiety and frustration he felt as he went through the process. This increases relevance because it assures students that it's okay to have the kinds of feelings of uncertainty and anxiety they are experiencing. Sam also could use this opportunity to share some tips for helping to alleviate those feelings.

Then Sam could hand out a worksheet with one of the following challenging problems and assign students the task of deciding how they would go about solving it using the model. This problem should be one of high interest, perhaps a mysterious or incongruous situation involving someone or something in the school (e.g., the school mascot is missing; all of the resources in the library have disappeared and the students have an assignment to research 20th-century scientists and their discoveries; a science experiment whose results seem to defy common sense).

Sam could ask the students to "mindstorm" (individually brainstorm) their ideas, write them down on a piece of paper, and bring their solutions to the library media center the next time they are scheduled to meet. In that next session, Sam could call on various students and write their responses on the board or transparency. This strategy allows students time to think about their answers and write them down, so if called on, they would feel more confident about responding. Or, Sam could have students meet in groups, choose the best three solutions, and have a spokesperson write them on a transparency to share with the class. This strategy addresses the various achievement motivations of his students.

It was obvious from their statements and behaviors that at least some of the students in this class had experienced research failure in the past. Rather than providing a forum for dwelling on past failures, it was important for Sam to establish a "clean slate" where students could begin again in a new school and a new year. It was also important for the students to become aware that they already knew and had used many of the skills they would need for research success.

Since a lack of research confidence seemed to be such an important factor with several of his students, Sam could end the lesson by telling the class that throughout the year he and their teachers would be working with them on a number of information problems. Sometimes they would be in the form of a homework assignment; sometimes they would be research projects. But the model they use would be applicable to all of these situations and he would be available to help them when they needed it. He might even set up specific help times when he would be devoted to providing additional assistance and one-on-one instruction to these students.

The suggested strategies would contribute to creating a motivating learning environment in Sam's library media center by addressing all three of the Motivational Goals for the Beginning Stage of research. You may have thought of other ideas that would be equally or more effective for this situation; be sure to include them in your Motivation Toolkit.

Motivational strategies like those above and throughout this book will not only help you to build your students' excitement for research, but they also are readily integrated into constructivist learning environments. We believe that creating a constructivist learning environment in the library media center will foster student motivation. The following section outlines our ideas about how the motivational goals and techniques we have recommended for information skills instruction fit into a constructivist learning context.

Creating a Constructivist Learning Environment

Constructivism, according to Duffy and Cunningham (1996), views learning as an active process of constructing (rather than acquiring) knowledge and views instruction as a process for supporting the construction of (rather than communicating) knowledge. It "places the learner at the center of a dynamic learning process" (AASL and AECT, 1998, p. 173). Kuhlthau (1993) found that the constructivist perspective's emphases on reflection, reconstruction, and interpretation provide a particularly useful framework for her research into the information search process.

Constructivist learning environments, therefore, are designed to engage each student in an individual, meaningful construction of knowledge, requiring him or her to (1) seek and organize information, (2) think critically and creatively, (3) plan and conduct learning and research activities, and (4) monitor his or her own understanding (Wilson, 1996; Jaeger and Lauritzen, 1992; McFadden et al., 1993; Savery and Duffy, 1995). All of these requirements are equally important in and directly related to information literacy instruction.

Constructivist learning environments:

◆ are student-centered and instructor-facilitated

◆ provide meaningful, authentic learning tasks

◆ demand application of critical thinking skills

◆ require interaction and collaboration

◆ foster responsibility for learning

Much of the constructivist literature describes the role of the instructor as that of "guide" or "coach." Library media specialists often serve in this role as they facilitate the information problem-solving process. We believe that one of the most important responsibilities of a coach is to motivate. On the next few pages, we'll take a closer look at each of the tenets listed above, examining some of their attributes, and see how they might relate to information literacy skills and our Motivation Overlay.

Figure 5-1. Constructivist Learning Environments Are Student-Centered and Instructor-Facilitated

Hallmarks of a Constructivist Learning Environment That Is Student-Centered and Instructor-Facilitated	Examples of Application of Constructivism to Information Skills	Examples of Applicable Motivational Goals and Techniques from the Motivation Overlay
■ Students are actively engaged and can draw on a wealth of prior knowledge (Callison, 1992). ■ Instructors model and teach metacognitive skills (Savery and Duffy, 1995). ■ Instructors are open to new approaches (Pitts, 1992).	■ Students learn new information skills by building on what they already know about finding information. For example, students discover that some of the same techniques for searching for print materials can be used in searching electronic resources. ■ Students are encouraged to solve information gaps, using a variety of information search strategies. ■ LMSs model ways to apply information skills to a variety of information problems.	The motivational goals from the Beginning Stage of research are important as you strive to generate interest in the research process. Techniques include: ■ stimulating curiosity by engaging students in a quest for knowledge and the need to know ■ establishing the importance of information skills by modeling enthusiasm for information exploration as well as the actual steps in the process ■ gaining interest by introducing a variety of approaches to the research process and remaining open-minded to alternative approaches by students

To create a constructivist learning environment that is student-centered and instructor-facilitated, your Motivation Toolkit must include techniques and strategies that stimulate students' interest and active engagement in the research process while you (1) model both the steps in the process and an enthusiasm for the process, and (2) remain open-minded to new or different approaches by students.

Figure 5-2. Constructivist Learning Environments Provide Authentic Tasks

Hallmarks of a Constructivist Learning Environment That Provides Authentic Tasks	*Examples of Application of Constructivism to Information Skills*	*Examples of Applicable Motivational Goals and Techniques from the Motivation Overlay*
• Based on the premise that learning takes place best in a meaningful context (Callison, 1992). • Uses authentic learning tasks and activities that draw on students' strengths and interests. • Students make sense of their world by logically linking pieces of existing and new knowledge, communication, and personal experience (Callison, 1992).	• Students use information skills to solve real-life information problems. • LMSs and teachers collaborate to integrate information skills with classroom assignments and activities. • Students synthesize information for research projects from a variety of resources.	The motivational goals from the Beginning and During Stages of research focus on establishing and maintaining the importance of information skills. Techniques include: • relating information problems to students' needs and interests • allowing students personal choices • linking information tasks to classroom activities and assignments

Information Power (AASL and AECT, 1998) recommends that information skills be taught in context, integrated with the curriculum. This parallels the constructivist premise that learning takes place best in a meaningful context where students tackle real problems and make real decisions. In a constructivist learning environment, your Motivation Toolkit incorporates techniques and strategies that increase relevance by (1) allowing students to share in the design of such a context by having choices, (2) selecting information problems of personal need or interest, and (3) linking information skills instruction to classroom activities and assignments.

Figure 5-3. Constructivist Learning Environments Demand Critical Thinking Skills

Hallmarks of a Constructivist Learning Environment That Demand Critical Thinking Skills	Examples of Application of Constructivism to Information Skills	Examples of Applicable Motivational Goals and Techniques from the Motivation Overlay
▪ Students are encouraged to develop new perspectives, create innovative solutions to problems, and test ideas against alternative views. ▪ Students reflect on learning outcomes and the learning process.	▪ LMSs provide open-ended information problems where students can construct a variety of possible solutions (Callison, 1992). ▪ Students work in groups to share perspectives and exchange ideas. ▪ LMSs allocate enough time for students to thoroughly explore information and reflect on information process (Pitts, 1992).	The motivational goals from the Beginning and During Stages of research are again important for creating a constructivist learning environment that generates interest in the research process and builds students' confidence in their research ability. Techniques include: ▪ creating positive anticipation by challenging students to think in new/ different ways ▪ maintaining students' confidence in their research competence by providing adequate time for successful completion of the research task and reflection on the process

Information skills require students to think critically. In a constructivist learning environment, your Motivation Toolkit should include flow-enabling techniques and strategies that encourage creative and flexible thinking and provide enough time for students to be able to explore information resources, think about their research topic, and reflect on their research outcomes and process.

Figure 5-4. Constructivist Learning Environments Promote Student Interaction and Collaboration

Hallmarks of a Constructivist Learning Environment That Promote Student Interaction and Collaboration	*Examples of Application of Constructivism to Information Skills*	*Examples of Applicable Motivational Goals and Techniques from the Motivation Overlay*
▪ Students work in teams for social negotiation. ▪ Students remain open to other perspectives and ideas.	▪ Students work in collaborative groups to share perspectives and exchange ideas (Callison, 1992). ▪ LMSs provide resources where students may encounter differing points of view.	The motivational goals from the During Stage of research help to maintain students' interest in the research process and reinforce confidence in their research ability. Techniques include: ▪ promoting inquiry through questioning and brainstorming ▪ allowing choices through variety of resources and opportunities to work individually or in large or small groups

Students high in need for affiliation gain much from working in teams. In constructivist learning environments, teamwork can be facilitated by using techniques and strategies from your Motivation Toolkit that foster questioning and brainstorming activities in which students share ideas and perspectives. Introducing students to a variety of information resources that offer varying viewpoints on issues and topics of interest also helps to maintain their open-mindedness and creative thought processes.

Figure 5-5. Constructivist Learning Environments Foster Responsibility for Learning

Hallmarks of a Constructivist Learning Environment That Foster Responsibility for Learning	Examples of Application of Constructivism to Information Skills	Examples of Applicable Motivational Goals and Techniques from the Motivation Overlay
▪ Students develop a sense of ownership for the learning problem and solution (Savery and Duffy, 1995). ▪ Students become "epistemologically empowered," believing the power of learning is within themselves rather than in external sources (Oldfather, 1992).	▪ Students gain the skills needed to be competent, independent users of ideas and information.	The motivational goals from the Beginning, During, and Ending Stages of research focus on building, reinforcing, and encouraging ongoing confidence in students' research abilities. Techniques include: ▪ offering a supportive learning environment that provides feedback on learning progress, reassurance and encouragement, and that allows students some control over their learning ▪ recognizing students' success and improvement by providing both motivational and informational feedback ▪ tying success to effort and skill through informational rewards

Nothing empowers people more than competence—possessing necessary knowledge and skills to be successful at a given task. For constructivist learning environments, your Motivation Toolkit should incorporate techniques and strategies that facilitate students' attaining research competence by helping them acquire information skills, providing opportunities for them to practice those skills, and offering them informational feedback and rewards that help them improve those skills and tie their successes to their effort and ability.

In summary, we believe that the application of the Motivation Overlay for Information Skills Instruction will promote and enhance constructivist learning environments. By using the techniques and strategies in your Motivation Toolkit, we submit that your students will feel:

- ◆ competent and confident about their ability to independently select and explore the world of information available to them
- ◆ satisfied that what they are learning can be used to solve problems and make decisions that affect their lives and the lives of others
- ◆ excited about the information they discover, the knowledge they gain, and the wisdom they share with others

Although we have only touched upon this belief in this chapter, we are currently working on a book that more fully explores the relationship of motivation and constructivism in an information literacy context for the 21st century.

Summing Up

As you come to the end of this book, we provide you with a review of some of the key points we hope you will take away with you.

- ◆ There are a number of information literacy models. However, none of them focus on the *motivational aspects of information skills instruction* from the instructor's point of view. That was the reason for writing this book.
- ◆ Addressing motivation is critical since motivated students are often more receptive to learning.
- ◆ Library media specialists do not have a *systematic framework* for incorporating motivational techniques and strategies into their information skills instruction. Such a framework must consider Kuhlthau's research on motivation of students as they enter and progress through the research process, as well as major motivation theories.
- ◆ Existing information literacy models may be summarized as *eight primary information skills across three time stages*. The eight information skills are Definition, Selection, Planning, Exploration, Collection, Organization, Presentation, and Evaluation. The three time stages of the research process are the Beginning Stage, During Stage, and Ending Stage.

◆ There is no lockstep process for research—which, in reality, is highly iterative.

◆ It is essential to learn as much as possible about the *incoming motivations of your learning audience.* We refer to this as the learner's "motivational profile." The motivational profile allows you to design information skills instruction that meets the motivational (as well as the learning) needs of students.

◆ For each stage of the research process, there are *motivational goals* that help guide the selection of motivational techniques for information skills instruction. Motivational goals describe the general feelings, attitudes, and motives you hope to achieve through your instruction. Motivational goals guide the subsequent selection of motivational techniques and strategies to incorporate into your instruction.

◆ One or more *motivational measures* may be used to determine if each motivational goal has been achieved. These may range from self-reports to observation of facial clues to increased question-asking to seeking out enrichment opportunities.

◆ The Research Stages, Information Skills, and Motivational Goals form the *Motivation Overlay for Information Skills Instruction.* The Overlay is not intended to replace but rather to be superimposed upon existing information literacy models.

◆ *Expectancy-value theory* provides the major theoretical basis to the Motivation Overlay. Students must both value and expect they can successfully achieve the research task.

◆ There are a number of *other motivation theories* that are important to the development of the Motivation Overlay, including need theories, curiosity, flow, attribution theory, and social learning theory.

◆ Keller's *ARCS Model of Motivational Design* also influenced the design of the Motivation Overlay. ARCS stands for Attention, Relevance, Confidence, and Satisfaction.

◆ *Motivational techniques* are broad methods, activities, and approaches that support the motivational goals.

◆ *Motivational strategies* are specific ways of implementing motivational techniques.

◆ A *Motivation Toolkit* identifies dozens of useful motivational techniques and strategies for planning, repairing, and enhancing information skills lessons at specific stages in the process. Each Toolkit may be customized to include those strategies that work best for you. Your Toolkit can expand year by year and should continue to expand over the years.

◆ The use of the Motivation Toolkit can help to create an information literacy skills program *within a constructivist learning environment* in which students are engaged in the meaningful construction of knowledge.

In Chapters Two, Three, and Four, we presented you with challenging situations to ponder. In this final chapter, we present several new challenging situations that include common problems which often require creative solutions. With a basic background in motivation principles and a Motivation Toolkit chock-full of great techniques and strategies, you now have the edge when facing such challenges. Please know that our responses to each ***What Would YOU Do?*** situation represents but one approach among a number of possibilities. Knowing what you know now, ***what would* you *do?***

What Would YOU Do?

? The school year has just begun and a new crop of tenth graders will soon enter your library media center. Not having had prior experience with these students on the middle school level, you were wondering what to expect. Earlier, you had done some preliminary research on the new students (conducting your *motivational profile*) by corresponding with the LMS at the middle school. She informed you that the new principal at the middle school had not been supportive of programs she wanted to implement in the past year and was not convinced of the benefit of working in tandem with classroom teachers to facilitate more meaningful research projects. (Believe it or not, there are still principals out there who expect LMSs to be islands unto themselves.) Thus, the middle school students had a tendency to "blow off" their visits to the library media center as unimportant. In your own experience at the high school, however, both the principal and teachers value teacher-LMS collaboration. You are about to meet the newcomers. What would you do?

! *When planning for students who have no prior track record with you or your library media center, the idea of conducting a motivational profile is a good one. By talking with the LMS from the middle school, you have gone right to the source . . . at least one of them. You might also benefit from interviewing several of the students to get the student perspective of their prior experiences as well. Based on your interviews with both the middle school LMS and the students, you may surmise that your greatest motivational challenge or goal will be to increase the **relevance** of utilizing the library media center for research projects. Since your high school supports collaboration with classroom teachers on projects, students will necessarily see the link between what you can offer and what they need to successfully accomplish their class projects. You can create additional relevance for learning information skills by showing how the same skills they need for their research projects can be used to make decisions on issues of personal interest to them. Naturally, you will also need to include some creative strategies to gain their interest initially and sustain it throughout the project.*

The next ***What Would YOU Do?*** will be a real challenge. You will have to think back to the theoretical underpinnings of some of the strategies presented in this book. But we think you are up to the task!

What Would YOU Do?

? Most of the fifth grade students in the library media center are absorbed in their research. They are using many of the information skills you have covered. Some are coming to you with interesting questions and some even appear to be in a state of "flow." They are in the During Stage of research when they are primarily exploring and collecting information. However, one of your students has several times raced to the window and looked around at what was going on outside. Upon inspection, there appeared to be nothing going on outside. Her behavior unfortunately has disturbed the flow of several students who have told her to stop. What would you do?

! *Remember our discussion of curiosity and flow in Chapter One? Curiosity is a state in which an individual has just the right amount of stimulation to want to explore for answers to the questions that aroused curiosity in the first place. Sometimes, curiosity can lead to a state of flow where students get so absorbed in their information exploration that they even lose track of time. You will also recall that flow requires an optimal level of challenge—not too much or too little. Likewise, curiosity requires just the right amount of stimulation to remain in a zone of curiosity. Too little may result in boredom; too much in anxiety. Everyone differs in this respect. What may be too little for one child may be too much for another. In this situation, you will need to make an assessment about the child who is disturbing the class. Is she racing to the window because she is attempting to relieve her boredom? (This brand of curiosity has no specific stimulus that triggered her exploratory behavior; she is simply seeking change.) Or, perhaps, has she become overstimulated and entered a zone of anxiety? You can help by reviewing with her the progress she has made on her research questions. This will help you to ascertain whether her exploration is proceeding at an optimal level of challenge that is neither too easy nor too difficult. Perhaps this student has come to a place that requires her to refine her original research questions. Once you have this insight, you can begin to help her organize her task into manageable chunks.*

Are you ready to tackle one last *What Would YOU Do?* This one addresses an all-too-common problem with young children in group situations.

What Would YOU Do?

?

Students are working on small group projects for a third grade assignment in your library media center. One student, named Brodie, appears to be isolated from the others. You have spoken with this child and have determined that he wants to be able to join his group. The group, on the other hand, is not being very gracious, and in fact is making Brodie feel that they do not want him as part of the group. From previous experience, you know that this child has enjoyed helping you with a variety of tasks in the center, from putting up posters to even dusting the shelves on occasion. What would you do?

!

*It seems that Brodie is suffering from an image problem with his peers. He apparently wants to be a part of his group even though the others are not responding. Unfortunately, we all know too well that children can be tough on each other. Beyond talking to the other students and insisting that Brodie be accepted, there may be an alternative strategy to consider. Think back to previous discussions on motivational profiles and make an educated guess as to what makes Brodie tick. You have a couple of clues. Brodie really wants to work in a group, plus he has shown a desire to help you with your everyday tasks in the library media center in the past. He feels comfortable with you and likes to be a part of what you do. This may indicate that Brodie has a **high need for affiliation**. He may also feel a certain amount of **power** from being the one you allow to do certain tasks in the center. Perhaps you could give Brodie a task that directly relates to the research project but involves all groups. For example, Brodie could be responsible for checking off completed student assignments, or helping maintain the CD-ROM encyclopedia. You could also announce to Brodie's group that you have selected Brodie to handle a task specific to that group's work. By giving Brodie responsibility for both whole class and small group tasks, you have not only appealed to Brodie's need for power, but have possibly helped to increase his status with his group so that they are more tolerant of him. This, in turn, addresses Brodie's need for affiliation.*

Now that you've tried your hand at the ***What Would YOU Do?*** motivational challenges, take a break and read how one of your colleagues tackled a challenge of her own in our final Motivational Makeover.

Motivational Makeover

Here is our final Motivational Makeover, submitted by Pamela Lipe Revercomb, LMS at Chittenango High School in Chittenango, New York, and a participant in our two-day summer workshop. Pam analyzed a lesson she planned with the U.S. history teachers in her school to introduce students to three electronic information resources in which they must find primary source documents. Although Pam's Lackluster Lesson Plan included some motivational techniques (e.g., a variety of media and materials linked to a classroom assignment), she diagnosed a number of problems with the lesson. After Pam's original lesson, we include her thoughtful, detailed analysis of the problems and what was needed to help solve them, followed by her new and improved version, her Motivational Makeover.

▶ Lackluster Lesson Plan

Audience: Eleventh grade

Topic: U.S. history

Instructional Goals: Students will locate primary source documents from a variety of computer-based sources, including the Internet, on topics relevant to U.S. history from 1776 to 1917. Primary source documents will be accompanied by a one-page written background information summary. Internet sources must be validated.

Information Skills: Definition, Exploration, Collection (primary sources), Evaluation (Internet websites)

Procedures:

1. Students will be seeking primary documents to supplement their textbook and classroom materials. The U.S. history teacher would like the students to use computer-based sources of information to find these primary documents. Classes will visit the library media center (LMC) three times during the fall semester—once for each of the following U.S. history units:

   - Constitutional Foundations (1776-1860)
   - Industrialization (1865-1900)
   - Progressivism and Imperialism (1890-1917)

2. During the initial visit, the LMS will demonstrate the use of three different computer-based sources. These will include:

   - *SIRS: Government Reporter* (online database)
   - *Gale's: Discovering U.S. History* (CD-ROM encyclopedia)
   - Internet

   The demonstration will be done in the LMC classroom, using the LCD panel and overhead projector. The teachers have requested that the lesson take no more than 15 to 20 minutes of class time so the students will have enough time for their research. Students will be in the LMC for two days only (for each unit).

3. Students will be given a "job aid" handout to accompany the demonstration. The job aid will include directions for using all three of the sources being taught. Students are expected to keep this job aid for use in their future research units in the LMC.

continued on next page

▶ Lackluster Lesson Plan (continued)

4. Following the initial demonstration, students will proceed to use the sources described to locate examples of primary documents. Students can use any of the sources suggested, so long as they find materials from the specified time period being studied on each visit.

5. Students print out or copy primary source material (e.g., letter written by a Civil War soldier) and write a one-page summary of background information about the document.

6. Students check validity of Internet websites by comparing information to similar information found in reference or other book encyclopedias in the LMC.

7. Materials and summary are collected and graded by classroom teacher.

Pam put a great deal of thought into the analysis of her Lackluster Lesson Plan. She started by taking a close look at her learning audience, creating a motivational profile. Based on her motivational profile, she was able to identify several problems with the lesson. Once she had a clear idea of what the problems were, she was able to rethink the lesson goals, content, and procedures. Here is her analysis.

Motivational Profile

Classes at Chittenango High School are moving away from being grouped as either Regents or Non-Regents. In response to the new New York State Standards, all students are expected to take (and hopefully pass) the Regents examination. Computer skills and competence levels vary in each class. Students requiring "resource" are included in the classes, receiving additional assistance outside of the class.

Students in eleventh grade should have used the LMC fairly regularly in ninth and tenth grades. They have had exposure to certain facets of the online databases being used (*SIRS: Government Reporter; SIRS: Researcher*), and some will undoubtedly feel they will be bored if they have to "hear it all again." Even though the focus will be on a new feature of the *Government Reporter* (Historic Documents), they will initially feel it is a waste of time to even see the demonstration. This may also apply to the Gale's CD (*DISCOVERING U.S. History*), whose counterparts (*DISCOVERING World History & DISCOVERING Biography*) are used extensively in ninth and tenth grade global studies. For the Internet portion, students usually do not mind having websites suggested, but will likely still complain about the demonstration method.

Probably only a third of the students in each class have access to the Internet from home computers. Another third may have used the Internet to some extent in the school setting. Others may have no familiarity with it at all. Of those who do use the Internet, most have used it primarily to "surf" and visit fun sites. For this reason, it is essential to generate and maintain interest in using the Internet as part of the research process. The Internet and the huge number of hits that can be produced when searching may intimidate students. Showing the importance of information skills in this process to help narrow search terms and interpret results will ease this type of frustration. In addition, *all* the students need to feel confident using and evaluating information found on the Internet. Strategies need to be employed to build and reinforce this confidence throughout the research process.

The demonstration method for this lesson has little potential for getting and maintaining the students' attention and curiosity. In addition, the classes are heterogeneous and lower-level students do not like to volunteer the fact that they are not "getting it" in a large group setting.

Problem(s) with the Lackluster Lesson:

1. *Too much at once (high potential for boredom, low confidence).*
   Especially for those students who are not familiar or comfortable with these computer-based sources of information, this is too much to absorb in one lesson. It should also take an entire class period, which is an issue for the U. S. history teachers. The teachers do not like the idea of taking an entire class period for research instruction. Long lessons will bore the students, who already have a grasp of these skills, and will add to the natural confusion and frustration of those who are *not* comfortable using the sources.

2. *Method of instruction (low potential for engaging attention + curiosity).*
   Demonstration by the LMS on the overhead can be effective; however, given the amount of information and directions required to cover all of these sources, and the time limit (15-20 minutes), the LMS will have to speak rapidly while jumping from one access method to another. There will be little time for re-teaching, questions, and elaborations to fit individual learning styles and needs.

3. *Prognosis for retention of material presented (not good).*
   The U.S. history teachers feel that once the students have received their initial instruction and the accompanying job aid, there will be no need for a review during the two later visits to the LMC (about six weeks apart). Most teenagers will not retain skills that are not used and reinforced for this six-week period. The other aspect of retention is physical. A large percentage of these students will have lost the job aid or be unable to recognize it in the chaos of their "notebook" (unless they are destined to become librarians and have already properly categorized their notebook).

4. *Evaluation of Internet website validity (lack of guidelines).*

   The U.S. history teachers' instructional goals include validating Internet sources. There is no instruction or model for the students to use to evaluate the accuracy of the information found on the Internet. Checking for validity in the book encyclopedias should prove the accuracy of the information. It would, however, be advantageous for the students to also evaluate the Internet websites more fully by using WebMAC© or a similar instrument created specifically for this assignment by the teachers and the LMS.

5. *Motivational problems in general.*

   Unless the teachers have done so in the classroom before the assignment, there is little here devoted to creating a sense of relevance or value for the students. There is a need for something to stimulate the students' interest in both the quests for the required primary documents and the value of learning how to do so.

Instructional Goals

The description of the instructional goals should include higher-level skills, such as analyzing and comparing information, interpreting historical perspectives, and evaluating validity of sources found on the Internet as a result of this project. These skills are representative of those expected in the new NYS Standards and Frameworks for the U.S. History curriculum. In addition, specific instructions or guidelines should be provided for the students to use in evaluating the validity of the Internet website information.

The "makeover" version of this lesson plan will ultimately have each of the three computer-based sources taught separately—one source for each visit to the LMC (six weeks apart). Each time, there will be about 15 to 20 minutes of instruction and a specific job aid for each source provided. The style of instruction will be different each time, in hopes of maintaining interest and curiosity.

Information Skills

Although there will now be three separate instructional lesson plans, the information skills remain basically the same for all three. There will, however, be less "Defining" and "Selection" for *SIRS: Government Reporter* and *Gale's DISCOVERING U.S. History* because the general use of these two sources has already been taught in ninth and tenth grades. For those lessons, the focus will be primarily on reinforcing or "building on existing knowledge and prior experiences" (Motivation Toolkit: "Beginning the Research Process") and relating that knowledge to the new part of the source being used (i.e., "Historic Documents" in SIRS or "Primary Documents" in Gale's).

When planning and team-teaching a lesson, my favorite model would best be described as a combination of the "Big Six Skills" and Kuhlthau's (1994) "Search Process." Because we will be starting at the Beginning Stage of the research process, I will introduce the lesson on two levels:

1. "You are here today to begin your quest to find primary source documents using the Internet." (Task Definition)

2. "Some of you may be feeling confused or uncertain at this point. You may still not be sure what a primary document is supposed to be. Others may be uncomfortable because they have never used the Internet before for this type of research (or at all!). We have planned this activity so it will be easy for every one of you to find this information, and you may also have some fun doing it!" (Confusion/Uncertainty ⇨ Optimism/Confidence).

For this lesson, it is expected that the students will move through the entire research process, selecting and focusing their topics, locating and collecting information, evaluating its accuracy, and ultimately presenting both their results and their evaluations of the websites used.

Motivational Goals and Strategies for Their Implementation (The Plan)

The revised lesson plan actually transforms the original Lackluster Lesson Plan into three separate lesson plans, with one plan and one computer-based source for each. In this makeover, I have prepared only the third lesson plan entirely in its new and improved format. In other words, the first two lessons will model new motivational wardrobe suggestions, while the third lesson will get the full makeover.

New Motivational Wardrobe Suggestions (First Two Lessons)

The motivational goals and strategies for their implementation will be the focus of change for the first two lesson plan revisions. The motivational goals to be incorporated into the revised plans for the first two lessons may include some of the following types of strategies:

◆ *Lesson #1: SIRS Government Reporter.* In order to generate interest in the topic and the research process for finding primary documents, it might be fun to wear a costume of some sort (e.g., pioneer prairie woman or Civil War soldier's uniform) and read a page from an authentic journal, diary, or letter.

◆ *Lesson #2: Gale's DISCOVERING U.S. History.* The importance of using information skills can be reinforced on the second visit by modeling an interest in finding primary documents from my own family history. There were a couple of prodigious inventors in my family, so I plan to share my personal experience of discovering this information, and show copies of some of their original patents.

Learning Assessment

In order to determine if instructional and information skills goals have been met, students will be graded on their completion of the following tasks:

◆ Produce a copy or printout of a relevant (time period 1890-1917 in U.S. history) example of a primary document.

◆ Complete the website evaluation form, including a source used to validate the website information.

Now it's time to unveil Pam's Motivational Makeover. We think you'll agree that the lesson, as it is now designed, is a good example of an information skills lesson with a high potential to excite her students about the research process.

▶ Pam's Motivational Makeover

Audience: Eleventh graders

Topic: U.S. history

Instructional Goals: Students will locate primary source documents from the Internet on topics relevant to U.S. history from 1776 to 1917. Students will use higher-level skills such as analyzing and comparing information, interpreting historical perspectives, and evaluating validity of sources found on the Internet as a result of this project. Copies of primary source documents will be accompanied by an evaluation of the website(s) using the instrument provided.

Information Skills: Definition, Exploration, Collection (primary sources), Evaluation (Internet websites), Documentation of Sources

Motivational Goals: To generate interest in the research process. To establish importance of information skills. To build confidence in research ability.

Motivational Measures:

Observation: Motivational goals should be met if students seem engaged and interested throughout the process and have little trouble producing the required products.

Discussion: A discussion of the website evaluations should offer an additional means of assessing the motivational temperament developed.

Lesson Plan:

1. Students will be coming to the LMC to use the Internet to find examples of primary documents to supplement their textbook and classroom materials. This will be the third time these classes have visited the LMC to use computer-based sources to find primary documents. Students will group in the LMC classroom and be introduced to the focus of this research lesson: using the Internet to find primary documents for the period in U.S. history. This time they will be searching for documents from the period in U.S. history described in their textbook as "Progressivism and Imperialism" (1890-1917).

2. It will be explained why information found on the Internet is not always accurate. Students will be given the task of finding examples of primary documents on the Internet and evaluating the validity of the websites used. If needed, a review definition of primary documents will be given.

continued on next page

▶ Pam's Motivational Makeover (continued)

3. Students will be put into four "search parties," based on their own evaluation of their Internet familiarity and ability. Hoping to make this fun and perhaps a little silly (difficult to accomplish in eleventh grade, but worth a try), the "search parties" will have names befitting a U.S. history theme. Students will be asked to choose which group they wish to join. All of the groups' names will be written and described on the whiteboard so students will have time to think about where they want to work. Search parties will be described as follows on the whiteboard:

   ◆ **EXPLORERS** (Need no directions and would love to enlighten the rest of us.)
   ◆ **INVENTORS** (Have a pretty good idea what to do, and would like some creative license in searching for and presenting results. AKA "surfers" in the modern world.)
   ◆ **COLONISTS** (Not sure where they are going or what they will find, but are willing to give it a try so long as they have a vehicle to get there with directions for its use.)
   ◆ **POSTMEN** (Want an exact website address and directions to get there.)

4. Because the Internet "pros" will be the first to complain when they arrive for this lesson, we hope to engage their curiosity first. We will ask which students feel they are truly competent at using the Internet and do not need any instruction; they would in fact prefer to instruct us on how to find information. These students will form a group in one corner of the room. Other groups will be described and students will form up. Hopefully, this fun style of describing varying student abilities for using the Internet will help defuse some of the initial anxiety for the students unfamiliar with the Internet. By having the students themselves choose their groups we hope to create some positive anticipation and expectations for success.

5. Once the groups are established, instructions will be explained. COLONISTS and POSTMEN will stay in the classroom for their "directions" and Internet "addresses" (i.e., a short demonstration of how to access the Internet using the Chittenango H.S. LMC computer network). However, anyone who chooses to may stay for a demonstration of how to get on the Internet and do a search via the Chittenango H.S. network. One or two suggested websites will also be shown, with instructions for finding links, opening and printing graphics, etc.

continued on next page

▶ **Pam's Motivational Makeover (continued)**

6. Students will be given a "job aid" type of handout to accompany the demonstration. The job aid will also have a few suggested websites for this assignment. Students will be encouraged to make suggestions for improving this job aid. This demonstration should provide a supportive learning environment that makes it easier to clarify the students' expectations. By offering these students the opportunity to ask questions and request reteaching, if needed, we can hopefully satisfy various learning styles.

7. Students will proceed to use the sources described to locate examples of primary documents. The LMS and classroom teacher will be available to assist students while checking on their progress and success during the research process.

8. The LMS will write LMC passes for students wishing to continue with their research during study halls or lunch periods. Individual appointments for assistance can also be arranged (during those times and/or tenth period).

9. Students print out or copy primary source material (e.g., letter written by a Civil War soldier). WORKS CITED information sheets will be made available so that students will be able to record their website URL address in the proper form.

10. Students check validity of Internet websites by completing an evaluation instrument provided by the LMS and the teacher. Completion of the instrument for evaluating the websites used will be required of all groups. Explanations for its purpose and directions for its use will be given as well. (If WebMAC© is to be used, permission must be obtained from Drs. Ruth Small and Marilyn Arnone.) One other source should be cited as proof of validity, such as a reference or other book encyclopedia.

11. Materials and summaries are collected and graded by classroom teacher. Students will discuss evaluations of the various websites used. Student suggestions for valuable websites will be recorded for future inclusion on the LMC webpage under "U.S. History: Primary Document Sources."

There is no doubt that Pam reached deep into her Motivation Toolkit and pulled out some great techniques and strategies to apply to her Motivational Makeover. As you can see, she has a number of strategies in her Toolkit that she added beyond those we suggested. She was able to justify her strategies based on what she knew about motivation. That is exactly the idea behind our Motivation Toolkit. We fully expect that what you have received through this book will be just the beginning of your own constantly evolving Motivation Toolkit. Pam's strategies were creative and fun, such as creating "search parties" based on students' own evaluations of their Internet familiarity and ability. We especially liked the way Pam paved the way for a "flow" experience by providing LMC passes to students who wish additional time to work on their projects. Throughout, Pam kept the all-important motivational principle in mind that students must both expect that they can succeed at acquiring information skills and find value in possessing those skills.

Final Thoughts

As we come to the end of this book, here's what we hope to leave with you:
- some renewed enthusisam for the important job you hold
- a sense that motivation is critical and can make a difference in the way that students perceive both their abilities to do research and the value of acquiring research skills
- a systematic way for you to think about designing motivation into your information skills lessons

Remember, this is just your "Starter" Toolkit. As you put new motivational techniques and strategies into your Toolkit, we invite you to share them with your colleagues. Send us your ideas so that we may post as many as possible on our motivation website. You'll find us at **www.MotivationMining.com**. We look forward to hearing from you.

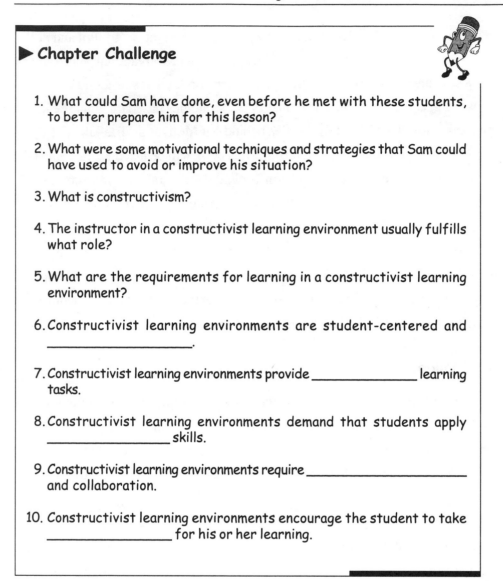

► **Chapter Challenge**

1. What could Sam have done, even before he met with these students, to better prepare him for this lesson?

2. What were some motivational techniques and strategies that Sam could have used to avoid or improve his situation?

3. What is constructivism?

4. The instructor in a constructivist learning environment usually fulfills what role?

5. What are the requirements for learning in a constructivist learning environment?

6. Constructivist learning environments are student-centered and _____.

7. Constructivist learning environments provide _____ learning tasks.

8. Constructivist learning environments demand that students apply _____ skills.

9. Constructivist learning environments require _____ and collaboration.

10. Constructivist learning environments encourage the student to take _____ for his or her learning.

▶ Chapter Challenge: Answers

1. Sam could have completed a motivational profile of this class, gathering information about their past research knowledge experiences and perhaps uncovering some of the attitudes they would bring with them.

2. Creating a nonthreatening learning environment, displaying more enthusiasm for research, relating information literacy to students' information problem solving, and mindstorming the solution to a challenging problem are a few of the techniques and strategies we thought of. You might have thought of others.

3. It has been described as an active process of constructing (rather than acquiring) knowledge and views instruction as a process for supporting the construction of (rather than communicating) knowledge.

4. The instructor in a constructivist learning environment usually takes the role of guide or coach.

5. In constructivist learning environments, students are required to seek and organize information, think critically and creatively, plan and conduct learning and research activities, and monitor their own understanding.

6. Instructor-facilitated.

7. Authentic.

8. Critical thinking.

9. Interaction.

10. Responsibility.

Reflection Points

Please use this page to record your ideas and special points to remember from Chapter Five.

References

AASL and AECT, *Information Power: Building Partnerships for Learning* (Chicago: American Library Association, 1998).

Belenky, M., B. Clinchy, N. Goldberger, and J. Tarule, *Women's Ways of Knowing: The Development of Self, Voice and Mind* (New York: Basic Books, 1986) p. 140.

Callison, P., "Naïve Conception in Science," PIMCES Summer Institute presentation at CSULB June 1991, cited in *The Construction of Meaning from Experience* (Louisville, Kentucky: National Council of Teachers of English [ED358 410], Nov. 23, 1992).

Duffy, Thomas M., and Donald J. Cunningham, "Constructivism: Implications for the Design and Delivery of Instruction" in *Handbook of Research for Educational Communications and Technology* (New York: Simon & Schuster, 1996), 170-98.

Jaeger, Michael, and Carol Lauritzen, "The Construction of Meaning from Experience," paper presented at the 82nd Annual Convention of the National Council of Teachers of English, Louisville, Kentucky, Nov. 1992 (ED358 410).

Kuhlthau, Carol, "Implementing a Process Approach to Information Skills: A Study Identifying Indicators of Success in Library Media Programs," *School Library Media Quarterly* 22, no. 1 (1993): 11-18.

Kuhlthau, Carol, *Teaching the Library Research Process* (Metuchen, NJ: Scarecrow Press, 1994).

McFadden, Anna C., George E. Marsh II, and Richard S. Podemski, "Trends and Issues in the 1992 Professional Education Literature," *School Library Media Annual* 11 (1993): 178-85.

Oldfather, Penny, " Sharing the Ownership of Knowing: A Constructivist Concept of Motivation for Literacy Learning," paper presented at the annual meeting of the National Reading Conference, San Antonio, Texas, Dec. 1992 (ED 352 610).

Pitts, Judy M., " Constructivism: Learning Rethought," *School Library Media Annual* 10 (1992): 14-24.

Savery, J.R., and T. M. Duffy, "Problem Based Learning: An Instructional Model and Its Constructivist Framework," *Educational Technology* 35 (1995): 31-38.

Wilson, Brent G. ed., *Constructivist Learning Environments: Case Studies in Instructional Design* (Englewood Cliffs, NJ: Educational Technology Publications, 1996).

Index

AASL and AECT, 3, 8, 21, 29, 39, 44, 55, 78, 162, 164, 191
ability, attribution to, 18
achievement. *See* need for achievement
Achievement Motivation Theory, 14-16, 39, 53, 134, 150
affiliation. *See* need for affiliation
anxiety, 6, 52, 99
    causes, 9, 16, 39, 82, 104
    techniques for reducing, 73, 90
applicability of skills, 52, 64, 66
    See also relevance
ARCS Model of Motivation Design, 22, 44, 169
assessment, 10, 58, 61, 104-5, 114, 183
    See also evaluation
atmosphere of acceptance, 14, 99, 102-4, 108-9
attention, component of ARCS, 22
attention-getting devices, examples, 7, 16, 41-42, 47, 66, 73-74, 90, 159
    See also brainstorming, curiosity
attribution theory, 18-20, 53, 126, 127
authenticity, 38, 44, 162, 164
    See also relevance

Bandura, Albert, 20, 29, 150, 156
Beare, Patricia G., 58, 78
Beginning Stage, 5-6, 10-11, 13, 24, 34-74
    theories applicable to, 13, 34-35, 66
Belenky, M.B., 157, 191
Berlyne, Daniel, 16, 29, 44, 78
Big Six Approach to Information Problem-Solving, 4, 125-126
Blumenfeld, P., et al., 44, 78
boredom, 16-17, 47-48, 179
brainstorming, 52, 66, 74, 84, 93, 101-2, 140-41, 166

Brophy, Jere, 19, 29, 56, 78, 99, 106, 120, 156
Brown, Paula, 101-2
Brunell, Mary Alice, 90
building on existing knowledge, 51-52, 66, 93, 160, 182

Callison, P., 163-66, 191
challenge, 15, 17, 45, 66
    appropriate levels of, 7, 12, 22, 39, 47, 58, 109, 173
Chapter Challenges, 26-27, 75-76, 117-18, 153-54, 188-89
Chemotti, Jan, 41, 103-4
choices, 74, 85, 96-97, 109, 139, 164
chunks, 7, 64, 68, 100, 109, 113, 180
clarity of requirements, 61-62, 66, 100
collaboration with teachers, 44, 50-51, 87, 94, 100, 132, 150, 164, 171
collection of information, 5-6, 24, 82, 95
competence, 57, 100, 105, 167
concept maps, 52-53, 66
Condry, J., 42, 78
confidence, 22, 34, 179-80
    building, 10-11, 24, 57-65, 74, 89, 97, 113, 116, 133-34, 159-60, 165
    maintaining, 11, 24, 99-107, 109, 166
    ongoing, 11, 24, 127-31, 146, 167
confusion, 90, 99
constructivism. *See* learning environments, constructivist
continued exploration, 24, 142-44, 146
control, 18-19, 57, 58, 61, 65, 66, 74, 96-97, 127
    See also locus of control, choices

criteria
    for assessment, 61, 66, 96
    for evaluating sources, 54-55, 138
    See also evaluation of resources
critical thinking skills, 105, 138, 162,
    165
Croak, Anne Lawless, 140-41
Crockett, Tom, 132, 156
Cronn, Katherine, 59-61
Csiksentmihalyi, Mihalyi, 17, 29
curiosity, 4, 16-17, 22, 33, 35-36,
    42, 44, 48, 66, 158, 163
    motivational theory, 16-17, 24, 53
curriculum
    mapping, 4, 50, 164
    using rubrics in, 61
    See also integration with
        curriculum

Davidson, G.V., 84, 120
Day, Marilyn, 111-16
Deci, E.L., 96, 120, 129, 130, 156
decision-making process, 53, 139,
    140
definition of information need, 5-6, 24,
    34, 55
difficulty, attribution to, 18
discussion, 84, 184
Donham, Jean, 52, 61, 78, 140
Downey, Sam, 2-3, 158-62
Doyle, Christina A., 3, 29
Duffy, Thomas M., and Donald J.
    Cunningham, 162, 191
During Stage, 5-6, 21, 82-116
    theories applicable to, 21-22, 24

effort, attribution to, 17, 18, 22,
    129-30, 146, 167
Eisenberg, Michael E., and Robert E.
    Berkowitz, 4, 29, 50-51, 78,
    125-26, 156
Eisenberg, Michael E., and Carrie A.
    Lowe, 3, 29
Emerson, Ralph Waldo, 21, 29

emotional responses, 4-5
    See also anxiety, confusion,
        frustration
encouragement, 7, 12-13, 66, 126
Ending Stage, 5-6, 124-52
    theories applicable to, 24
enrichment opportunities, 7, 15, 142-44,
    146, 147
enthusiasm, 7, 21, 48, 49, 66, 130,
    159
epistemic curiosity, 16, 44
Epp, Tongay, 38-39
evaluation of product/process, 4-6,
    24, 124, 125-26, 136, 138-40
    as critical thinking skill, 138
    by instructor, 126, 132
    instruments, 104-5, 186
    of sources, 3, 54-55, 104-5
    requirements for, 61, 96
    See also self-assessment
expectancy for success, 12-13, 22,
    57, 98-99, 127, 144
expectancy-value theory (E-V theory)
    11-13, 22, 24, 34-35, 53, 57,
    131, 144, 169
exploration of information resources,
    5-6, 9, 24, 82, 99
extrinsic motivation, 18, 20, 22, 42,
    147, 150
    See also rewards

failures, past
    effects, 12, 19, 113, 116
    overcoming, 19, 107, 113, 160-61
    See also learned helplessness
feedback, 17, 19, 22, 66, 89, 105-6,
    107, 109-10, 167
    See also recognition, rewards.
Fitch, Lauren, 138-40
flexibility, 65
    See also control, choices
Flip It! Model, 4, 30
flow (motivational theory), 17-18, 24,
    53, 165

frustration, 12, 68, 90
Frymier, Jack R., 105-6, 120
fun, 46, 85, 116

Gardner, Howard, 39, 78
Geneen, Harold, 104, 120
goals
    instructional, 10, 69
    motivational, 10-11, 23-24, 34,
        66, 109, 146, 163-67
Good, T.L. and J.E. Brophy, 94, 120
Gottfried, A.E., 17, 29
Grady, Barbara, 97
Gray, Ann, 69-74
group activities, 7, 15, 64, 84
guidance, from instructor, 7, 127
    See also feedback, help
        mechanisms
guidelines, need for, 100, 109
    See also clarity of requirements

Hanks, Kurt, 46, 78, 156
Harter, Susan, 42, 78
help mechanisms, 64, 100, 102,
    103-4, 109
Hierarchy of Needs, 14, 53
humor, 48, 85, 93-94

independent users, 102-3, 158, 167
inexperienced researchers, addressing
    needs of, 58, 64-65, 86-87
information gap, 16, 44
information literacy, 3-4, 8-9, 11, 49,
    55, 64, 168
information motivation, 9, 23
information skills, 4-6, 10-11, 23-24,
    50, 93
inquiry, 90-91, 109, 166
    See also questioning
instructional motivation model, 21-22
    See also ARCS Model
integration with curriculum, 7, 94,
    109, 164
    examples, 106, 143-44
    See also curriculum

interest, generating, 10-11, 24, 35,
    37-48, 163, 183
    maintaining, 24, 83-91, 137-38,
        166
    See also attention-getting devices,
        curiosity
interests, of students, 12, 55-56, 66,
    116, 164
internal attributions, 18-19, 58
    See also attribution theory, locus
        of control
intrinsic motivation, 16-17, 19-20, 21,
    22, 42, 44, 58, 96, 129-30
I-Search, 85, 86

Jaeger, Michael, and Carol Lauritzen,
    162, 191
Johnson, D.W., and R.T. Johnson, 15,
    30
Joyce, Marilyn Z., and Julie I.
    Tallman, 85, 86, 120
just in case/just in time, 42

Kehoe, Louise, 40, 78
Keller, John M., 22, 30, 44, 47, 78,
    99, 169
Keller, John M., and Bernard Dodge,
    42, 79
Kopp, Thomas W., 79
Kuhlthau, Carol, 1, 4-5, 6, 8, 9, 10,
    21-22, 30, 42, 45, 48, 52, 57-
    58, 64-65, 79, 82, 89, 99, 120,
    124, 125, 132, 156, 162, 168,
    182, 191

Lankes, Anna Maria D., 132, 156
learned helplessness, 19, 53, 107, 110
learning audience, 9-10, 23, 113, 150,
    169
    See also motivational profiles
learning-disabled students, 113, 116
    See also low-achieving students
learning environments
    constructivist, 16, 158, 162-68,
        170
    student-centered, 23, 162-63

learning environments (*continued*)
　　supportive, 14, 22, 57, 59-61, 66,
　　　　82, 102-4, 116, 126, 167
learning styles, 48, 83-84, 135-36,
　　173, 180
　　See also need theories
Lepper, M. R., and Melinda Hodell, 42,
　　79
lesson plans. *See* Motivational
　　Makeovers
lifelong learning, 23, 44, 142
Limpert, Susan, 149-152
Locke, John, 81-82, 120
locus of control, 18-19, 53, 116
　　See also attribution theory
Loewenstein, G., 16, 30, 44
low-achieving students, addressing
　　needs of, 20, 99, 111-16, 180
Lowenthal, Barbara, 156
luck, attribution to, 18
Lumsden, Linda S., 12, 30
Lyles, Dale, 38-39

Macrorie, Ken, 86, 120
Make It Happen!, 85, 121
Maslow, Abraham H., 14, 30
McClelland, David C., 14, 30, 39, 134,
　　150, 156
McFadden, Anna C., George E. Marsh
　　II, and Richard S. Podemski,
　　162, 191
Miller, Harvey, 132, 156
Miskal, C., J.A. DeFrain, and K.A.
　　Wilcox, 12, 30
mnemonics, 85, 109
Model of the Search Process, 4-5
modeling of behaviors, 7, 20-21, 49,
　　94-96, 109, 128, 163-64
Motivation Overlay for Information
　　Skills Instruction, 10, 22-25, 36,
　　124, 168, 169
motivation theories, 8, 11-22, 23-24,
　　34-35, 53, 105, 168-69
Motivation Toolkit, 23-24, 35, 66, 109,
　　124, 146

motivational assessment measures, 10,
　　69, 169
Motivational Makeovers, 69-74, 111-16,
　　148-52, 158-62, 176-87
Motivational Moments, 35, 39, 40-44,
　　51, 54-55, 59-61, 62-64, 85-86,
　　87-89, 90, 94-95, 97, 101-2,
　　103-4, 135-36, 137, 138-41,
　　143-44
motivational profiles, 21, 23, 159, 169,
　　171, 175, 179-80
　　See also learning audience
motivational strategies, 7-8, 22, 23-24,
　　36, 47-48, 58
Motivational Style Quotient (MSQ), 6-
　　8, 12, 15-21
motivational techniques, 8-9, 23-24, 35
　　See also Motivation Toolkit

Neary, Diane, 42-44
need for achievement, 14-15, 39, 93
need for affiliation, 14-15, 64, 88, 93,
　　107, 134, 166
need for power, 14-15, 93, 127-28,
　　134
need theories, 13-16, 24, 53
Nelson, Bob, 128, 156

observation
　　as motivation assessment measure,
　　　　10, 69
　　as motivation strategy, 20-21, 128
Oldfather, Penny, 167, 191
opportunities
　　for applying skills, 144, 146, 167
　　for enrichment, 7, 15, 142-43,
　　　　146, 147
　　for success, 100, 109
organization of information, 5-6, 24, 82

Pappas, Marjorie L., and Anne E. Tepe,
　　4, 8, 30
participation, 15, 48, 69, 90, 138, 157,
　　162-63
Pathways to Knowledge, 4, 8, 30

patience, 105-106
peer-tutoring, 7, 15, 127-28
performance standards, 61
persistence, 105-6, 107
personal narratives, 86
Pitts, Judy M., 163, 165, 191
planning a search strategy, 5-6, 24, 34, 45, 51-52, 55
Plotnick, Eric, 4, 30
Poole, Charlotte, 46
positive anticipation, 40, 47-48, 66, 165
power, need for. *See* need for power
praise, 7, 18, 129-30
    See also recognition
presentation of information, 5-6, 24, 124, 125, 137-38
problem-solving approach, 10-11, 38-39, 44, 52, 66, 164

questioning, 7, 16, 22, 42, 90-91, 109, 138-40, 166

Rappaport, Ellen D., 54-55
recognition, 39-40, 105-7, 109, 136-37, 146, 167
    See also rewards
references, 29-31, 78-79, 120-21, 156, 191
reflection, role of, 125, 131-32, 146, 162, 165
reinforcement, 21, 22, 53, 107
    See also recognition
relevance
    of assignment, 41, 48, 55, 64, 164
    component of ARCS Model, 22
    of skills, 50, 55, 61, 93-94, 109, 128, 168, 171
    See also integration with curriculum, interests, value of information skills
Research Process Model, 4, 125
    See also Stripling, Barbara K., and Judy M. Pitts
research stages, 5-6, 10-11, 24
    See also Beginning Stage; During Stage; Ending Stage

responsibility, 7, 41, 136, 162-63
Revercomb, Pamela Lipe, 176-87
rewards, 18, 20, 39-40, 106, 128-29, 136-37
    See also recognition
Rhoads, Mary-Elizabeth, 138-40
Romance, Renee, 40
Rotter, J. B., 18, 30
Rowe, Mary Budd, 91, 120
rubrics, 61

satisfaction
    component of ARCS Model, 22
    promoting, 11, 24, 97, 131-41, 146
Savery, J.R., and T.M. Duffy, 162, 163, 167, 191
School Librarian's Workshop, The, 40, 78
School Library Media Activities Monthly, 87, 120
selection of research topic, 5-6, 24, 34, 45, 55
self-assessment, 138-41, 146
self-determination, 23, 44, 57, 58, 96, 126
Seligman, Martin E.P., 19, 30
Sikop, Kendra, 87-89
Small, Ruth V., B.M. Dodge, & X. Jiang, 47
Small, Ruth V., 22, 31, 36, 47, 99, 120, 130
Small, Ruth V. and Marilyn P. Arnone, 16, 31, 48, 186
Social Learning Model, 20-21, 24, 53, 96, 128, 150
SOS (situation-outcomes-strategies), 23-24
Spitzer, Kathy, 61, 128
Stafford, Debbie, 136-37
stages of research, 5-6
    See also Beginning Stage, During Stage, Ending Stage
stimulation, 16, 21, 48, 173
Stipek, Deborah J., 12, 31
Stripling, Barbara K., and Judy M. Pitts, 4, 31, 125

teamwork, 15, 134, 166
   See also need for affiliation
time allocation, 7, 17-18, 45, 64-65,
   125, 165
Time Continuum Model, 21-22, 31
Tinker, Pam, 135-136
Toumbacaris, Barbara, 95
tying success to effort/skills, 17, 22,
   127, 129-30, 146, 167

value of information skills, 9, 10-11, 12-
   13, 24, 50, 53-54, 55-56, 66,
   93-97, 109, 160, 163
variety, 83-85, 86-87, 109
   of presentations, 85, 125, 137-38
   of resources, 86, 89, 164, 166
   of skill levels, 179
Vroom, Victor H., 11, 12, 31

Waldron, Anna, 143-144
Warner, Richard L., 87, 120

WebMAC©, 104-5, 181, 186
Weiner, Bernard, 18, 31
Weintrub, S., 33, 48
What Would You Do?, 68, 110, 147,
   170, 171, 172-73, 175
Whittaker, Susan, 62-64
Wielt, Jennifer, 59-61
Wigfield, A., and J. Eccles, 99, 120
Wilson, Brent G., 30, 162, 191
Wlodkowski, Raymond J., 21-22, 31,
   39, 93, 121, 123, 156
Wlodkowski, Raymond J., and Judith
   Jaynes, 47, 65
Wright, Janice, 51-52

Yucht, Alice H., 4, 31

Ziglin, Janice, 85-86
Zorfass, Judith M., 85, 121

About the Authors

Ruth V. Small, PhD

Ruth is associate professor and director of the School Media Program at the School of Information Studies at Syracuse University. She holds master's degrees in library science and education and received her doctorate in instructional design, development, and evaluation from Syracuse University. Her teaching and research focus on the applications of motivation theories to a variety of information-based learning, work, and virtual environments. Over the past 15 years, she has consulted for dozens of government, corporate, and educational organizations in the United States, Europe, and South America. Ruth was named 1996 "Professor of the Year" by the graduate students of her school and is the 1997 recipient of the AASL/Highsmith Innovative Research Award.

Marilyn Arnone, PhD

Marilyn is president, New Product Research and Development, and cofounder in 1984 of Creative Broadcast Associates, Inc., the parent company for Creative Media Solutions, which specializes in television and multimedia production. She is coproducer and director of research and evaluation for a nationally televised educational program for children. Her research interests have centered on exploring children's motivation (particularly curiosity) and learning in interactive multimedia environments. She is adjunct professor at Syracuse University's School of Information Studies. Marilyn received her master's degree in education from Harvard University and her doctorate in instructional design, development, and evaluation from Syracuse University.